The Truth About Networking: Strategic Business Networking, The Facts You Should Know

This book gives you more than just "tired and true" networking tips. What's more, it helps you understand how and why networking works in both business and interpersonal relationships, and provides real insight about interacting with one another. You will pick up many new ideas and use them to build your own network of contacts, increase your client base and expand your market. No matter what business you're in, this book can help you uncover new business and customers. It should be right up there on the bookshelf with all your other business reference books!

The techniques in this book are business saving. It covers new and novel approaches to marketing that are smart and effective.

It addresses problems that many people have with meeting people, building relationships, and projecting a professional image. In an era where cradle-to-grave job security is a thing of the past, it is beneficial to continue building relationships throughout your career. Excellent Advice for any Networker and a wonderful resource for everyone. Even if you don't think you need networking skills for your work, trust me, you'll get a lot out of this book. It is filled with specific, lively examples that spark your imagination and build your confidence that you too can be a great conversationalist. Excellent resource.

Table of Contents

Sales Techniques - Setting Goals for Gaining Clients by Networking

Do your sales techniques include business networking to gain new clients? Studies show that one of the best ways to meet potential clients is through professional networking. Yet how often have you returned from a business networking event wondering why you bothered going, since you never seem to get any new business?

You'll be more successful at your next business event if you set goals for yourself beforehand. Think about what you want to accomplish, and write down your objectives for the event. Your goals might include:

-Meet new potential clients: Your goal at a networking event is to make contacts - not to make sales. When you meet someone new who has potential for you, don't try to sell to them at the event. Arrange to meet at one of your offices, or at lunch or dinner.

-Meet someone specific: If possible, get a list of people who will be attending the event. This way you'll know in advance whom you want to meet. You can arrange for the host or hostess to introduce you, or just go up to the person and introduce yourself.

-Broaden your sphere of contacts: Networking is a great way to gather information. You may meet people who have no need for your product or service. Remember that you don't connect with only one new person. You have the opportunity to connect with this person's sphere of contacts. You increase your chances of getting clients when you are referred by a common acquaintance.

-Strengthen relationships: You may meet people who have never used your services before. Suddenly their business needs have changed, and they are looking for what you offer. Spend time finding out their needs, and see if you can provide a solution.

-Practice your networking skills: If you find networking challenging, don't worry. You don't have to be the life of the party. That's probably not realistic, and you'll set yourself up for failure. But you can decide that you want to meet three new people over the course of the evening and converse with them for approximately 10 minutes each.

Set achievable goals for yourself. Then when you reach your goal, reward yourself by spending a few minutes talking to a colleague or have something good to eat. After all, you've reached your goal!

You are invited to use these sales tips to help you set achievable goals for you next networking event.

You're also invited to receive a free report: "Breakthrough Communication Skills" packed with powerful tips for business success, at http://www.ImpressforSuccess.com when you join my Communication Capsules newsletter.

Would you like to attract new customers, increase sales, and boost your career? Visit here for simple How-to Guides that give you immediate results. http://www.goldmansmythe.com/howto.html

From Lynda Goldman, business communications and etiquette consultant and author of 30 books, including How to Make a Million Dollar First Impression.

Lynda Goldman

Selling Accessories Online Using Social Networking For Fun and Profit

Social networking is not only being used by people today to get in touch with friends and relatives in every corner of the world or making new friends along the way. In truth, social networking is now being utilized by business-minded individuals to sell their products for profit.

If you check out social networking sites on the Web, you can see that some of those people on your network are selling their own products and services to the rest of the online community. In fact, there might even be hundreds, or even thousands of others on the service doing the same thing.

One hot selling product in the market is men and ladies accessories. Whether its bags, blings, jewelries, or even make-up, you can be sure that the market for this on the Internet is quite high, since everyone is quite conscious on how they want to look out in public. If you are interested to set one up for your own, there here are some tips that you might find useful.

Tip # 1: Look For A Social Networking Site

You need to look for a social networking site that offers features that will fit perfectly with your online business. Rather than concentrating on sites that only offers extensive network of contact, personal customized profiles, and a way to find and communicate with other people on the community; you might want to settle down in sites that has other features like blogs, bigger storage space, RSS feeds, guest books, chat rooms, and so on.

Tip # 2: Set Up A Blog

You need to create a blog that will showcase all your products to the rest of the online community. Rather than posting your accessories on you profile page, a blog site would give you enough room to provide informative content to your customers, a good layout to integrate pictures of your accessories, and so on.

Blog sites are also well-suited for a business function, since your visitors can directly comment on your products if they find it to their liking or not. In fact, these feedback areas can be used to place orders online without the need of setting up complicated ordering systems that will only be a hassle to maintain.

Tip # 3: Improve Your Popularity

Now that you have the site and information ready for your potential customers on the Web, it is now time for you to start with a little Internet marketing strategy to boost your site's accessibility for bigger profit.

Start off by adding more people into your contact list that will serve as your downlink for the business. While you're at it, you might want to create a group so that people can sign up and join to become your permanent customers in the venture. You can also trade links with other members that features their own businesses in the online community to improve your reputation and online coverage.

http://conbuzz.com -- Social Networking

Vanessa A. Doctor from Jump2Top - SEO Company

Vanessa A. Doctor

SEO Cheats - Video Networking Your Way Into Google's Top 10

At the time of writing, the major search engines are giving priority to videos in their search results. For example, if I had a fairly new site that was ranked number one in Google for a particular niche keyword, it is likely someone could beat my site to the top spot in one day. All they would need to do would be to submit a video to Youtube that had the same keyword my site ranks highly on, in its title/description (regardless off the videos content). That is the power that videos currently posses over search engines.

So how can you harness that power in an effective manner? Lets go through an extended example and examine this.

The guide to a top ten position - through videos

Example: Robert and his E-commerce PC monitor shop

Robert has a website that specialises in selling PC monitors. Shiny flat screens capable of incredibly high resolution. You know the ones the I mean. His site has a Google page rank of two and is receiving fifty unique visits each day, which he is happy with for now. His main problem is that the sites conversion rate (sales of the monitors) is negligible. Perhaps one a week. So Robert decides to take the initiative and look on the internet for helpful SEO techniques. After reading many worthless articles he happily stumbles across this particular one (forget the time travel implications) and it gives him a warm feeling inside.

He reads that by making a video about his website in which he really promotes his products he could conceivably double his visitors and sales. He follows the steps it suggests and the next day he finds that his website's name has 3 new spots on the top twenty list on Google. Rapidly both his visitors and conversions increase and Roberts life is changed for ever.

What Robert Read.

That's all well and good for Robert and the above is a completely plausible scenario. Infact it has happened for many people. But how can video sites benefit you? Lets now go over what steps Robert would have had to have taken in order to achieve multiple spots on Google's top 10.

Creating Your Video

Keep your video under ten minutes in length so it accepted by video sharing sites that have length restrictions. It does not have to be a true video - that is to say the content could be text or possibly just audio, as long as it is saved as a video file (avi..) The content should promote your site and preferably the products you are selling on your site. Try to mention your web address a few times. Now save the file 3 times - each must be different quality (thus different file sizes), and save them with different names. We will examine why you have done this shortly.

Submitting Your Video.

Before you submit your video there is one more important thing to do. This is to create a new text document and write into it your websites name, and then write into it three differing descriptions of it (including a few choice products). Next, search for all the video sharing websites that (not p2p) you can find (Youtube, DailyMotion, Odeo - there are dozens more). Now we come back to the three different video files. Every times you submit your video and a description, rotate through your three different files and texts. Google will like the variations. A lot. It is a fairly time consuming process, but hopefully well worth it for you.

The Waiting Game

Here's the easy part. It will only take a day for Google to list some of the new videos you have submitted. They should be ranked highly when any of the keywords in the description(s) you wrote for them are searched for. From these videos, not only will your site receive a boost in Google's rankings (the more links for high Google rank pages the better for your site), the people who watch the video should be interested in your product so may very well look at your site after watching and possibly purchase something they saw.

That's all there is to it. It does not always guarantee multiple high ranked listings, but with a little bit of video magic, it quite easily could.

Nicholas C Smith is the project manager at Breakfrom Limited, who specialise in affordable ecommerce solutions and general web design knowledge and advice.

For more information and advice visit http://www.breakfrom.com

Nicholas C Smith

Serious Business Networking

As they always say It ‘s not what you know, it ‘s who you know. □

Of course just knowing people doesn ‘t necessarily get you the job, or the promotion, or the contract you wanted, but it certainly can help; so long as people don ‘t think you are using them.

It ‘s true that networking is extremely important, so finding new contacts is the key to your continuing success; you need to learn out about networking meetings or events in your area.

Before you go to an event you should think about what you want to achieve. Who will be there? Decide who you would like to meet and what information you would like to take away. This will ensure that you remain focused and have a successful meeting.

Use your Capsule Profile from the "Presentation Statements ' that we discussed in the self-marketing section of the website. http://www.your-career-change.com/personal-marketing.html

You have about thirty seconds to get a person 's interest or you lose your chance. Planning this beforehand is absolutely essential. You need to sell yourself before you can ask for the information or contacts you want.

Consider the impression you 're making and don 't repel people by your (bad) jokes or (bad) manners or the way you smell (tobacco, garlic or aftershave / perfume).

It isn 't always easy to talk to people, but if you don 't at least try you may lose out on an opportunity. Keeping a positive attitude and keeping smiling will increase the positive results. People enjoy networking with interesting, purposeful individuals.

Dress for Success (http://www.your-career-change.com/Dress-for-success.html) at a business networking meeting as you would if you were going to an interview or a meeting with your most important client.

If you spend all your time with contacts you 've already made, you limit the value of the event; so the majority of your time should be spent meeting new people. Networking meetings enable you to expand your contact list if you use your time well.

Do your best to remember the new contacts ' names; we only tend to hear our own name when introductions are made so repeating their name will help you to remember it. And they like to hear their own names. Furthermore people will be most impressed when you remember their name the next time that you meet.

Only collect a lot of business cards if you have good reason for each one and they allow you a follow-up action. Make notes on the back so you know where they came from and what follow up you intend to take.

Although it's crucial to talk about yourself, you don 't want to spend all of your time explaining what you do. Find out what the other person does. People love to talk about themselves and it will give you time to understand them and how you may be able to help them. If you can help them, they will be more likely to help you.

With over 25 years running businesses; as a Career Coach and Consultant in many sectors; Peter Fisher is well placed to guide job seekers through the steps needed in order to achieve that all important new position.

He has personally coached thousands of individuals to career success. These years of experience are distilled into all the essential facts and actions you must complete in order to achieve your own success. He is very clear that you shouldn 't be misled into thinking of acing interviews □ or finessing □ your way into a business; the most sustainable and fulfilling roles are gained through understanding your own specific needs and creating your strategy accordingly. http://www.your-career-change.com/personal-marketing.html

You can learn more about his dynamic and comprehensive approach to career change, with every page dedicated to helping serious career changers if you go to http://www.your-career-change.com/index.html

Peter Fisher

Sharpen Your Business Networking Skill To Grow Your Small Business

Most people become lax at maintaining their professional business network when they 've worked with a company a while. With the constant rounds of mass layoffs, having a dead or outdated business network can mean business suicide to even the most skilled expert.

Whether you've been laid off and are looking for work or are a small business owner trying to grow a business, connections are crucial for business success. But it's not so much who you know as who knows you. And that means networking effectively should be one of your priorities. Here are a few tips to help you get the results you seek from business networking.

- Before you go to a networking meeting, be prepared with a goal. Who do you want to meet? Why are you there? Have a conversation icebreaker ready to get to know the right people.

- Don't reserve every seat and act like a grump if someone unfamiliar wants to sit there. Welcome the opportunity that a stranger presents. They may be your next prospect.

- Treat referrals like gold. Contact the referral within a day, if possible. Let the referrer know how things went.

- Online, your email creates the first impression just like your physical presence does at face-to-face meetings. Be the business professional that you are.

- Any email you send has the potential for being forwarded to an untold number of people. Before you press the "send" key, give your message the "front page" test. Ask, "How would I feel if this made the front page of the newspaper?"

Denise O'Berry is a small business expert who helps small business owners grow their business with less effort. Additional business networking tips may be found in her guide -- "101 Nuggets to Power Up Your Schmooze-Ability" at http://www.deniseoberry.com/101tips

Denise O'Berry

Six Obstacles to Networking and How to Overcome Them

Networking is like so many things in our lives - exercise, eating more fiber and less fat, quitting cigarettes, saving money, writing goals - that we know are not only good for us, but are the keys to success. We know because we've occasionally done them enough to see and feel results, but we didn't keep up with it. Or we've seen our friends doing these things and enjoying great health. Or we've seen the news articles about the studies that prove these things are beneficial. We've even read the books by the experts and celebrities who clearly spell out these actions and habits as the reason for their wealth, health, and happiness.

We know all this, and we know that networking is a vital business development activity and an important life skill, so why don't we do it? Because there are obstacles in the way of our success, some obvious and some so subtle that we don't know they are there. Of the six major OBSTACLES to networking, nearly all of them are created inside our own minds. Therefore, it is simple (but perhaps not easy) to change our thinking and to remove them.

The six reasons why we don't network are:

· Misconceptions · Dislike · Having no Purpose · Not Knowing How · No time · Shyness

Misconceptions Are you holding onto false beliefs about networking that are mostly negative? You think it's just schmoozing, or that it's all about selling, or it's only for outgoing people? Did you try it once and when you didn't get results, or didn't feel comfortable, you decided it wasn't for you?

The basis of any of these fallacies is that you believe it doesn't work or that it won't work for you. This error in thinking that is very easy to disprove. Simply look at the millions of business people who are successful because of the relationships they built through networking. Read books by Dale Carnegie, Harvey Mackay, Andrea Nierenberg, and Keith Ferazzi to be convinced of the value and the principles of networking.

Dislike Do you dislike networking because you don't feel like selling or being sold to? Do you avoid it because of other people and their poor networking skills? Have you had negative experiences that caused you to have misconceptions about networking?

If you avoid networking because you don't like the way other people do it, you need to radically shift your thinking from annoyance and dislike of these people, to compassion and seeing an opportunity to help them change bad habits. And just like daily life outside of networking, we need to simply deal with those few who don't have good skills and keep searching for the right people to build relationships with. If you've had negative experiences with networking, you need to research your organizations much more thoroughly. We don't eat raw food for the rest of our life because we burned our hand on the stove once. Avoiding networking because of other people is cutting our noses off to spite our faces.

Having No Purpose Do you see networking as an endless series of pointless cocktail parties full of vapid conversations? Is your contact database not growing or even shrinking as people move away? Do you only network when it's time to change jobs or when business is slow?

If you do not have a strategy and a long-term outlook, you will network based on short-term need, such as losing a job. This can be very unsatisfying because desperation is unattractive. Experienced networkers will avoid your "help me now and I'll forget you later" approach. Harvey Mackay calls it "digging your well before you are thirsty." Your purpose in networking is to build a vibrant, growing, and responsive assortment of relationships you can count on, and who can count on you. The development of mutually beneficial relationships will make every conversation important and purposeful, there will be no more pointless chitchat. Instead, you'll see each time you make contact or converse with someone as another vital but small contribution to the networking structure we are building

Not Knowing How Do you feel okay with meeting people, but wonder what to do next? Or you are building your contacts, but don't see results from it. Are you unsure what kind of conversation is appropriate if you're not going to sell?

If you lack technique or are unsure how to take networking from the early stages of meeting someone to a deeper relationship that is going to create value for both parties, then you may create in your own mind the perception that networking doesn't work. Or that it's okay for other people who don't have money for advertising, but that it's not necessary for you.

Networking begins with basic social skills such as having conversations that are other-centered. We may feel comfortable in purely social settings like soccer games or birthday parties where we can talk about our children or the happy occasion, but we believe that business networking occasions should be all business. Remember that businesses are run by people, and those people have families, interests, and personal needs. Getting to know someone first is not only perfectly acceptable in the business world, but is the basis of building mutually beneficial relationships.

Once you're comfortable with learning about people for themselves and not as a prospect or sales target, the next step in knowing how to advance the relationship. The most effective and easy way to do this is to give first. Send them information, an invitation or even a referral for business. They will gladly work with you in return.

We sometimes think that we should automatically know how to network just by virtue of being in business, but this is the one topic where there is a gaping hole in our education and training. Financial planning companies are notorious for bringing in their new associates, giving them detailed FINANCIAL training, no networking training, and then sending them out to network one of the most difficult industries there is. The range of skills that are needed in networking include conversation skills, the ability to perceive and fill other people's needs, organization, and a clear process for creating a return on the investment of time. This range of techniques requires study and application, like any complex skill.

No Time to Network Are you ready to network, but you find you just don't have the time? Do you pencil in networking events, but then have too much work to do and can't leave the office?

There are only two reasons you don't have the time to network. Your life may truly be so complicated with jobs, second jobs, childcare, or elder care that you literally work 16-hour days every single day of the week. But, if you watch one single hour of mindless television a day, you are just making excuses to not network. You don't lack the time; you just don't want to make the time.

Any busy person who discovered a new passion or a fun new hobby has found that it is possible to find the time when you strongly want to do something. Suddenly, your schedule opens up, you find new efficiencies, or you are able to reprioritize. If you're not able to do that with networking, revisit your beliefs and your purpose. The time will almost magically appear if you are clearly focused on the value of networking.

There are also ways to be much more efficient and effective with the time you spend networking. Instead of very general events with a random group of people, take time to research exactly whom you need to add to your network and target your networking time accordingly. A leads group is also a time-efficient way to network because it is focused on giving and receiving referrals. You may even want to create your own networking events and activities. This would be a larger investment of time, but the return is much greater when you are the organizer and host.

If you have a short-term perspective, you will feel that the time invested isn't paying off. If you think you're wasting time, you won't spend it. But if it is a long-term project that will compound, it is much easier to find the time to invest. We so often have to deal with the urgent tasks that aren't important, instead of networking, which is not urgent but very important.

Shyness Do you feel like you can't be a good networking because you are an introvert? Or do feelings of shyness hold you back from networking? A majority of people in the population report feeling some shyness at different times. These feelings contribute to the misconception that only outgoing people are good at networking. Having no clear purpose and needing to work on our social skills can compound feelings of shyness, which are basically a lack of self-confidence. Preparation and planning can create confidence, which causes us to be successful which make us more confident.

There are also networking events that are better suited for a more introverted person. Large, non-agenda mixer meetings can be difficult for anyone if you are unfamiliar with the group. Use the buddy system and focus on smaller, more personal events to build your confidence.

Conclusion Think carefully about your excuses for avoiding networking in relation to these six common obstacles. Nearly every one of them is founded in the way we think. Once we've removed these obstacles that come between ourselves and our goal of effective networking, our success is assured. Apply diligence to make sure you're not allowing bad thinking habits and doubt to creep back in. From now on, it's simply a matter of time and consistent effort.

Beth Bridges is the Membership Director of the Clovis Chamber of Commerce in California. She has helped thousands of people get connected through hundreds of networking events with the Chamber and other organizations. Learn more about growing your networking, speaking, and personal development skills at http://www.NetworkWithILG.com Get great networking tips, tricks, and strategies at http://bethbridges.blogspot.com

Beth Bridges

Small Business Networking: An Overview

Small business networking is very important to success. You, the computer consultant, are entrenched in the professional services business, which revolves around relationships and thus networking with a large number of people.

You need to make small business networking of the utmost importance when starting your business and take things slowly. You will not get a large number of clients, nor will you get clients that need you immediately when you go to your first big networking event, even though you could come away with five or six really good prospects.

The Key Word Is Contacts □

Small business networking offers the opportunity to find good client contacts, but it also allows you to find people that know people who might need you or perhaps have similar business philosophies that would be good to know in the future and might bring you more business.

Once you make contacts of any sort, make sure you follow up and have meetings, proposals and sales calls. This type of small business networking is much better than trying to find emergency, one-shot clients. You can forge paths with people that are or can put you in touch with steady clients capable of long-term support. Even if every networking event doesn't produce a large number of clients, it can help you get referrals that will improve your ability to conduct productive small business networking.

The key in small business networking is to have a lot of different leads and many contacts at the same time. Some will be ready to jump into long-term client status and some will not at different stages and different times, but keeping in touch with all of them will help you stay in contact with a lot of potential and actual business.

Client contacts and referrals will help you find long-term steady clients that will help your business last for the long term. Even though going to small business networking events may seem a waste of time, you could gain exactly the types of contacts and even clients you need to really drive yourself forward.

Joshua Feinberg, co-owner of Computer Consulting 101, gets computer consulting businesses more steady, high-paying consulting clients. Now you can too. Just sign-up now for your free access pass to these field-tested, proven computer consulting secrets at Computer Consulting 101 .

Joshua Feinberg

Small Talk Savvy For Effective Small Business Networking

Small business owners rely upon networking to meet potential clients, to boost their visibility in the business community and to make connections that can lead to more connections and greater business opportunity. And, what does effective networking rely upon? Small talk.

So it's important to understand small talk savvy basics and to not rush your relationships.

This is key: small talk is all about process. You start with a simple Hello □ and move forward ; taking small, logical conversational steps. Yet, so often people want to skip steps. They want to go from Hello □ to Thank You for Your Business. □

Treating small talk strictly as a business skill rather than an important all-around social skill is a mistake. Your life can be so much richer if instead of bluntly asking for the sale, □ you first connect with the people you meet.

This is especially true in dealing with other women. Men may be more comfortable getting right to the point, but I believe that women like to be valued a bit for who they are, and not just as another business prospect. Once you 've really listened to another person and chatted with them long enough to understand what their needs are (this may take more than one meeting), then certainly let them know that your business product or service is just the resource they 've been looking for.

So take small talk in steps and stay open to the great potential that small talk engenders. Do this and small talk will connect you to people who:

Support your personal and career goals Energize and uplift you Teach you new things Present you with opportunities to help others Expose you to new activities and ideas Expand your understanding of different kinds of people Grow you ability to hear others □ Know other people you should meet

And the list goes on and on. It 's tempting to think of small talk in relation to short-term goals. But, use small talk wisely and there should be no shortage of people who want to connect to you for the long-term.

Melissa Wadsworth is a conscious communications expert and the author of Small Talk Savvy (a Borders bookstores exclusive). She speaks about effective small talk to various business groups. Melissa also uses her 20 plus years as a PR professional to create dynamic and effective PR/Marketing copy for clients. Learn more by visiting her at http://www.melissawadsworth.com If you contact her and mention this article she will email you her "Top Ten PR Tips."

Melissa Wadsworth

Social Engineering Bots Trick Social Online Networking Folks to Giving Personal Information

There is now a new artificially intelligent identity theft group using software called "cyber lover" and this program is one, which flirts with people online. Unfortunately, it is now being used by Russian hackers in the hopes of using social engineering to trick people into giving out personal information or luring them to a website that will give their computer malware. The program is able to flirt online either through e-mail or in chat rooms and dating websites.

The person you think you're flirting with is not a human and all rather an artificially intelligent program that mimics human behavior in a flirtatious way. After the individual target thinks they are flirting with a real person, the program tells them to go to a blog or a personal website on a social network, which then delivers malicious code to their computer.

Just one copy of CyberLover, can carry on 10 different relationships online in 30 minutes and its victims cannot distinguish it from being a human.

One might say that the old clichÃ©; Don't Trust Anyone; now needs to be rewritten: Don't Trust Anyone or Any Computer. Apparently, the identity thieves are getting to be quite good at their trade and they are using the best trick of all, social engineering. Folks who are lonely and looking for friends on the Internet are much more vulnerable to such attacks and sophisticated Mal ware can spread the virus through social networks like wildfire.

The government authorities now say that the US Internet users must be very careful and they recommend the following things to protect your self online:

Never give your personal details to anyone over the Internet. Consider using aliases/fake names on social networking sites and when chatting online. Carefully monitor the online behavior of your family members and educate them of the dangers. Ensure you have up-to-date AntiVirus and Anti-Spyware installed, with real-time and behavioral protection

Of course, this may not be enough, because if a user is lured to a website to watch a video or look at a picture, even if the antivirus or anti-spyware catches it, the user may still open up a dialogue with the computer, and later be handed off to an individual to steal their identity. Something to contemplate in 2008.

"Lance Winslow" - Online Think Tank forum board. If you have innovative thoughts and unique perspectives, come think with Lance; http://www.WorldThinkTank.net/ . Lance is an online writer in retirement.

Lance Winslow

Social Media & Networking For the Anti Social

Have you ever leaned back in your chair after Facebooking, blogging and twittering the afternoon away and wondered where the last 5 hours went? Upset now that you have to work late to do what you should've been doing while you were "socializing?" The time and effort involved with social marketing has turned us a bit anti-social and downright selfish with our time. So what is a busy person who knows the importance of social marketing to do?

Before Web 2.0, running a successful business meant doing your work right, on time, on budget consistently. Now with Web 2.0 in play, we also have to broadcast on the Internet how, when, where, what, and why we're doing it.

Social marketing outlets include blogging, Twitter, Facebook, MySpace, LinkedIn, and YouTube. Do you have to engage in all of them to reap the benefits from social marketing? If the staff, time and resources allow, then sure. But for the majority of us, these things are commodities to be spent wisely. Choosing which social networking "club" to join is key to how successful your social marketing campaign is.

Locate your target audience and run with that social crowd. Twitter, Facebook and the like all have reputations for attracting a specific type of audience and some are broader than others. However, uploading a video on YouTube for an older baby boomer market would probably miss the mark. But this demographic does use email so an invitation to read and subscribe to RSS feeds from your blog is the way to connect with them.

For B2B or service professionals, LinkedIn is the place you want to hang out. Reminiscent of chamber of commerce functions, this online version allows members to network with peers in their industries, past work places and former classmates. Ask questions, answer questions, give and receive recommendations, etc. Filling out your profile is often the most time consuming aspect of using LinkedIn.

Facebook and MySpace are excellent places to instigate a conversation and bow out quickly while the masses carry on without your presence. Build your friend or fan network, make a daily post and let them weigh in on your latest news. In all reality, what they say about your company or product carries more weight than anything you could say about it anyway. It's an objective way to get their opinions and change your strategy accordingly.

Monitor your social status to ensure good things are being shared. Reputations are made and ruined on the Web in just a matter of hours. That housewife in Peoria who is raving or complaining about your customer service isn't just talking to her neighbor. She's talking to 550 "friends" around the world.

Regardless of where or how you engage your customers in social media, be meticulous about your spelling and grammar. Twitter's 140-

character limit doesn't leave much room for error and mistakes reflect poorly on your business. Twitterers can also use applications with built-in spell check like Twirl. Proofread twice, read it out loud to yourself and make the subject relevant- a topic that will compel people to respond.

A sentence or two here, a post or blog there. As long as you choose the right outlet and method, social marketing has the ability to go a long way toward building your brand and increasing your business. Social networking doesn't have to take up 5 hours of your time and it doesn't require overcoming any anti-social tendencies. In fact, that's the beauty of it. Proceed confidently into that social marketing arena, introduce yourself, make the rounds, and stir up some conversation. And that parsley in between your front teeth? No one will notice.

About the author: Brenda Galloway owns the Kansas City-based marketing communications firm, Write Essentials LLC, specializing in Web and print copywriting that builds interest and increases conversion rates.

Want more ideas and tips to make your marketing copy work harder and be more persuasive? Then visit http://www.writeessentials.com to sign up for "The Write Idea" newsletter.

Brenda Galloway

Social Networking - A Marketing Tool

Social Networking is the greatest marketing tool available to virtual businesses today. How do we gain presence otherwise? The storefronts that gain presence in the brick and mortar world are reached by different vehicles of transportation and communication than those in the virtual world. Discussing how brick and mortar businesses gain presence will help us realize what we should be doing to gain this presence for virtual businesses.

Social networking defined is the practice of increasing individual as well as group contacts. Although social networking has been practiced for as long as society has existed, the effect is much more powerful on the web. The Six Degrees of Separation theory holds that any person on the planet is able to be connected to anyone else on the planet "through a chain of acquaintances that has no more than five intermediaries" (Wikipedia, 2009). Based on this concept, the rate at which one can connect to anyone else on this planet via social networking on the web is accelerated.

Let us now discuss the differences in which business presence is gained in both the brick and mortar and virtual worlds. First of all, storefronts in the brick and mortar world can be seen by several vehicles of transportation and communication. For instance, it is common to browse storefronts while taking a stroll, waiting for a bus, or exiting a bus and walking home. Maybe you have a specific shopping day and you a take family or friends shopping. You will probably browse several stores, new and old. This is one way for the local business to gain presence. What about non-local businesses?

Cities with several options for using public transportation help people get from point A to point B true, but also expose people to more advertisements and storefronts than in their neighborhoods. Many times a trip using public transportation requires that a transfer to another bus or train be necessary in order to reach a final destination. What does this mean? That's right; people see more advertisements and more storefronts.

Also popular offline is word of mouth. Word of mouth would have to rate as number one as a marketing tool. Word of mouth usually comes with something more than just advertising...client's opinions. This can make or break a business, but you should have nothing to worry about if you are good at what you do and you are honest. Good reviews can bring an organization many clients in the future and it doesn't stop there, word of mouth equals more word of mouth. Increasing reviews means an increase in business.

In fact, there are only two ways in which businesses gain presence on the web; one is through the search engines and the other is by social networking, which is the foundation of cultivation. Online business owners do not have people strolling across the web or exiting buses. The closest thing to strolling is browsing. People browse the net all of the time. Search engines on the web can be compared to two things, strolling and the yellow pages. It all depends on whether you are browsing (general search such as hardware stores) or searching the search engines (a more specific search such as Joe's hardware store).

Social networking online is comparable to word of mouth offline. In fact, a friend of mine named Richard Butler AKA the Success Coach describes social networking for business online as "word of mouse." According to Misner (2002) Word of mouth marketing "is the world's best known marketing secret." Misner maintains that business professionals take word of mouth too lightly and some think it has to do with customer service. Although customer service is important and may save your hide in negative situations, word of mouth is more than customer service.

According to Misner (2002), the happy client does not talk to as many people about his experience as the unhappy client. The unhappy client can speak about his bad experiences with literally dozens of people. Misner states that word of mouth must become an important part of marketing and can be achieved by practicing and realizing three important things. Firstly, it is important to diversify your networks. This means getting out of your cave and gaining presence in the community. Secondly, you should develop your contact spheres and this is as simple as networking with businesses that are non-competitive with your business. In fact, these businesses will compliment each other and may help the others gain referrals. For example, Misner refers to a florist, a photographer, a jeweler and a travel agent as the wedding mafia because one referral becomes four. Lastly, realize that word of mouth is more about cultivating relationships than hunting for clients. In other words; you should focus on quality rather than quantity.

There are approximately 200 social networking sites available on the web. Approximately fifty of those sites are particularly focused on business. Examples of social networking sites focused on business are Delicious, Digg, Twitter, LinkedIn and StumbleUpon. Word of mouth starts with you so registering with these sites is highly recommendable. Become your businesses most valuable asset and let the mouse do the talking.

References

Misner, I. (2002). Word of Mouth: The World's Best-Known Marketing Secret. Retrieved May 23, 2009 from http://www.entrepreneur.com/marketingideas/networking/article53188.html

Wikipedia (2009) Social Networking. Retrieved May 23, 2009 from http://en.wikipedia.org/wiki/Social Networking

Simone Brady

Social Networking - A Quick and Easy Way to Build Your Business

Today with fast communication and easy access to information through the web, people are relying more and more on social networking. It is cheaper, easier and gets results by generating more traffic, site exposure and interest.

Not so long ago businesses used to hire a sales work force to network and cold call in order to get their names known. Some would send out flyers, advertisements or even CDs through snail mail " AOL being one of the biggest to capitalize on that market. I think we all remember those monthly CDs waiting for us in our mailboxes when we came home from work. But, all that advertising takes a lot of time, money and extra man power which smaller business just cannot afford. Social networking makes these mundane and expensive advertising tasks much easier. Imagine achieving BETTER results at little to no cost and with you in complete control.

Some of the first websites to use the Social Web were Del.icio.us and Digg. The idea was very simple ; bookmark the sites and articles you like or even add the links to your webpage. When you have thousands of people doing this across the country, results just soar. It becomes your own direct response web marketing tool and it takes little effort. What you need to do to get involved is simple " put your website profile on a few search network sites and then wait. That is it.

Putting up your profile on sites, such as Fast Pitch. LinkedIn, FaceBook, Merchant Circle, Jigsaw and many others will enable you to list classified ads, post events or press releases and promote your website. It only takes a few gos to get started and the more sites you are linked to, the larger and more diverse your web community will be. By being part of a network, you can also promote your products and services to a database of clients quickly and easily without the extra costs and hassles. You might even attract net surfers and clients in fields you would not have originally advertised.

TeamWork Builds Web Success

The Web Success Team specializes in building and marketing direct response websites that take full advantage of the latest developments on the Internet. The Team has an arsenal of effective web strategies, online tools and proven techniques to promote your products and services. And we 'll show you ways to increase the amount of qualified traffic to your site through the expanding social web □ and how to convert visitors into buyers at a high rate of return.

Your website can become an effective marketing hub for your business. To learn more about the power of Direct Response Web Marketing, log on to http://www.websuccessteam.com/whydirectresponse.htm

Contact the Team today for a complimentary consultation at http://www.websuccessteam.com/contactus.htm or email Bob Speyer at bob@websuccessteam.com To your web success!

Robert Speyer

Social Networking - Discussed Thoroughly

Did you ever wonder why Facebook, Friendster and MySpace are becoming more and more famous? Did you ever ask yourself what these things are and why are they well-known all over the world and people are very much into it? This is because they can contact friends, gain buddies and renew relationships.

These are examples of what we call the social networking services. It is defined to have a good turn on building online communities to the people who have the same interest and shares common activities with each other. They are the kind of services that are very much interested in exploring the attentions as well as the goings-on of people.

What do you need to know about social networking service?

Most of these services are based in the web. They provide a lot of ways for the users to interact through the internet. These are the e-mails and the instant messages that we are currently using.

This is one way of encouraging people to adopt new ways and go halves with a lot of information at hand.

These are used by millions of users around the world.

The first social network service that was first initiated are the e-mails and the instant messages and so with the websites, but up until now, it is constantly changing for better development through the use of technologies.

The earliest social networking services are those who have lots of certain categories to choose from such as former classmate that will connect with all friends.

The idea of it came from the strange thought of linking the computers for the benefit of a media-related interaction of people.

The first launched social networking services websites are commenced as a generalized online communities, these are said to focus on taking away people to interrelate with each other through the use of chat rooms where they can be able to share their own personal information and anything they can talk to under the sun.

From a simple building of communities concept up to the notions of bringing people together, social network services began to do well as an advantage business component. Business minded people are now trying to use the social network services as first-rate strategy to expand target market and increasing sales.

From social network services as a good strategy for business, it plays an important role in the society for connecting big and small industries and organizations. They can be able to reach a large scope of audience in which have the same interest and passion. It can let like minded community to have benefits from each other.

The typical structure for social networking service is that, they can agree to a customer to create their own profile that will be in accordance to their personality. The users can upload pictures and customize what they wanted as well.

It is made because of the goal of giving each others benefits from it.

A social networking service is a good way to share common interests and affiliations of the same people.

Social networking is a means of communicating with anyone in the web. To know more about social networking, checkout http://socialbiznetwork.com

Michael J Paetzold

Social Networking - How to Communicate Effectively Using Twitter and Other Social Media For Business

Social media and social networking using sites like Twitter and Facebook have become some of the hottest buzz words on the Internet today. For those solo professionals and entrepreneurs who work at home, one of the major benefits of social networking is having the opportunity to communicate with people from all over the world using the power of the Internet.

People from all walks of life and from all around the world are hanging out by the millions on places like Facebook and Twitter.

Of course meeting new people, whether it's in your own neighborhood or across the globe, means using effective communication. Particularly if you're using the Internet to get the word out about your business, you need to communicate effectively because you don't have the same nonverbal cues others do face-to-face or even over the phone.

The main thing to remember when you're communicating about your business to others online is this: always keep your "audience" in mind. It's not about you. Every one of us is tuned into our favorite radio station: WIIFM (What's In It For Me?).

With that in mind, here are my top 3 tips to communicating effectively to market your business using the power of social networking:

1. Build relationships

Just like when you build relationships in person, you have to have a conversation. Ask people about them and their interests. Share a bit of yourself (not just your business) to gain that all-important "know, like, and trust" from people reading your posts.

2. Offer Value

People will continue to flock to you if you offer them some value. Provide links to free resources you come across, articles, others' blog posts you found interesting, or other information relevant to what your audience wants/needs.

3. Answer Requests

Very often people will post surveys, ask questions and in general look for feedback on their ideas, websites, etc. Take a moment or two to help someone out. Then when you need help, others will be there for you in return.

I personally have experienced many benefits to building relationships online. As a result of following these tips, I've quickly learned that sites like Twitter and Facebook can be highly effective for business and help savvy entrepreneurs make more money and have fun too while social networking.

I've personally had a lot of success using Twitter right from the beginning. I've been invited to speaking engagements and sold my products and services all using Twitter. I'd like to invite you to learn the basics of what it takes to succeed by marketing your business on Twitter here:
http://www.communicationtransformation.com/twitterbasics.html

Regardless of the method you choose, effective communication with your clients and prospects is the key to making your business successful. The first thing you need to communicate-- and continue to communicate -- is your credibility. Without credibility, your business will go nowhere. With it, you'll automatically attract new clients and see positive cash flow.

I invite you to discover what you need to know about Credibility and Cash Flow now. Visit http://www.CredibilityAndCashFlow.com to get your free e-course that will help you customize a credibility plan for your business and get you more clients, more business and more money.

Felicia J. Slattery, M.A., M.Ad.Ed. is a communication consultant, speaker & coach specializing in training small and home-based business owners effective communication skills so they can see more cash flow now.

Felicia Slattery

Social Networking - How to Have WordPress Blog Posts Auto-loaded to Facebook Notes

Facebook is at the top of the list whenever Internet marketers mention social networking. The news feed alone makes Facebook a worthwhile place to be. Now you can share your blog posts with your Facebook friends without a single keystroke. By setting up this blog feed, your friends will be just one go away. That means hundreds, even thousands of opportunities for new contacts to access to your information.

Setting up a blog feed is easy. Just follow these simple steps:

Log into your Facebook account. Go to your Profile Page. In the center of the page is the status box where you can tell everyone what you are doing. To the right of the status box, just beneath the blue rectangle that reads POST, you'll find a tiny link saying, "Settings" and a tiny asterisk beside it. Go Settings. Under Stories Posted by You, is a line reading, "You can automatically import activity from YouTube, Flickr, and Other Services to your profile." Go Other Services. Go on Blog/RSS, and a new box will open up. Place your blog's RSS feed link in the box. In WordPress, the blog RSS feed URL is http://YOURBLOGNAME.com/?feed=rss2 Go Import.

Now when you post to your blog, the entire post will come up in the Notes of your profile page and a news feed will announce the note. You can go to the Notes page and go on SHARE to tag friends in the Note. You can also place the link for the Note into your Facebook groups' pages.

And now I'd like to invite you to get my free 30 Lesson ecourse "How to Support Your Family Using 1 Non-fiction Book." The course is delivered by email, on audio segment each day. To get yours, go to http://RoseyDowFreeStuff.com

Rosey Dow is CEO of Experts in Focus--http://expertsinfocus.com

Rosey Dow

Social Networking - It's a Party, Stupid

Somewhere along the line, people appear to have become confused about what socializing really is. What is it that has me all worked up?

Here it is, I was mucking about on Twitter the other day and yes, I'll admit it, almost every day and I noticed that all of the updates in my profile were attempting to market stuff to me. Even worse people appeared to be simply placing links in the "What are you doing?" updates.

Frankly I don't like that. In fact, if you are doing this, stop right now and get with the program. I have to admit that sometimes I've done the same thing but I quickly realised that this was not the forum for pitching to people . This is a place for sharing stuff - my stuff, your stuff, good stuff, weird stuff. I think you get the idea.

Quite a few of us have been online for some time, and we see how people get upset when you are spamming the social sites. There is another way to use these sites, it's a bit radical but I think you will like it. How about you use them for the purpose they were created... to socialize with people.

I mean the name kinda gives it away don't you think?

So let's take a look at what Social Networking means:

It means that you get to Network with like minded people. People that you would like to socialize with. That's pretty simple isn't it? If someone sounds interesting, or fun or is passionate about some of the same things as you, you get to network with them. Simple.

Social networks are like being at a party. People come along to have a good time, share some of their thoughts and maybe some of their inspirations. They are there to have a giggle, join a group and basically be entertained.

Look, here is an example:

A little while ago I was talking with a friend about something that I'd seen or heard on Twitter. She asked me, as she had just started up her own blog, if she should be "doing Twitter too. I warned her that Twitter and other social networking sites can become quite addictive. I warned her that she could find that she was no longer getting any work done and that she had gone into the Twitter Twilight Zone! This happens because it's so much fun! This happens when we create real networks, when we really begin to socialize.

My definition of Twitter Twilight? Well... it's just like text chatting on your cell/mobile phone. You get so totally in the flow of typing short little messages, little bytes of your life and you start using all sorts of short cuts (sometimes I can't even read back what people are trying to say!) and then all of a sudden the phone rings. WHAT! A cell phone that actually rings... my God what is this world coming to?

Look, I totally understand. We get into the flow when we are socializing, it's so good hanging out with other people who are doing the same kinds of things that we love to do and before we know it - four hours have blasted by and we didn't even notice! Been there? I sure have.

Social networks are the same, so you have to structure yourself a bit.

Here are a few tips:

Treat them like a real party and only talk about what you would talk about at a party . Start to build relationships and make a point to meet people. Also, really use your profile page and more information section. You can put all you want in there... but make it look good, make people want to hang out with you. Then, just like at a real party, once you have met a few people and checked each other out. Once you know what you have in common, if it seems like a good idea you can invite them over to your place for a BBQ (oh, I mean, invite them to check out your blog). This isn't the place to start selling them and pitching to them either. Your blog is full of great content, lots of value, terrific inspiration. They will just want more once they have seen it, right?

If you've done the socializing stuff well and built a good relationship and then provided them with terrific value then it will be just a natural flow for them to sign up for your newsletter. No pressure, no sell - just the natural course of events.

Something else.

This is important for you to understand.

Your auto-responder service is not the only list you have. I know you think it is but think about it for a minute. Every single social networking site you are part of and that included video sites, everywhere you have friends, this is also a list.

Think about it. If in your social sites, you simply socialize with people... it can't help but happen that one day you will be working on something new, something big that you will be wanting to promote. So, you naturally write a blog post with a little video as part of what you are working on and it turns out fantastically. You know that people are going to love it... and it's role is to get people to sign up for more videos which will later sell those very same people!

So what do you do? You totally explode to your friends on the social site:

You get excited and you share that excitement with your friends, it's only natural. It could read something like... Oh my Goodness... Sal... you just have to see this very cool video I just posted to my blog... retweet please LINK!@)

What do you think is going to happen? I'll tell you what, all of a sudden, after nights of working late and little sleep... after months and moths of dreaming about it and realizing you don't really have a list at all... you check your email and... and it would seem that you have 305 notices saying "You have a new Subscriber!"

That is how it works. That is how you relax and learn to socialize, really socialize and just have fun. Put in some real effort, be sure to fill your profiles in. Use your REAL name, your REAL picture and find some great stuff to put in there about you and your family and your life.

The business stuff can come later. Enjoy the party a bit first, find the sites and scenes that suit you best and then just be natural, go with the flow and start making some real contacts.

Many people wish to own their own business and the growth of Internet Entrepreneurship has seen a massive increase in the number of people needing information on Internet Marketing. For more information about how you can learn what you need to know to create a successful online presence and create an Alternative Livelihood for yourself, just visit the Alternative Lifestyle Site blog and go on the WEST Program banner. http://www.AlternativeLifestyleSite.com/blog

Cate Ferguson lives in Australia and has been involved in the personal development and empowerment field for many years. Cate is also passionate about the environment and is in the process of creating a sustainable lifestyle for herself and her family. Cate writes articles and blogs, makes videos and other resources for those looking to learn more about the environment, sustainable and alternative lifestyles, climate change, permaculture and Alternative Livelihood.

Cate Ferguson

Social Networking - Protecting Kids

Children today invariably use the social networking sites to keep in touch with their friends and relatives spread across the globe. They create accounts on various social networking sites and start interacting with each other. Children create their account without finding out the proper details about the social networking sites. In most cases, they take the words of their friends and provide all the details that they are prompted to. This in turn leads them to problems such as cyberbullying, identity theft, and put computer security on stake.

To avoid problems of this sort, it is very important that the children or the parents first find out the details about the security settings about the networking site. At the same time, it is equally important the parents also find out the details about the security settings that the children have chosen for their profiles in the online world. After the parents have properly understood the security policies of the social networking sites and also checked the security settings chosen by the children, the next step is to educate the children about social networking safety. Parents must educate children about the dangers of entering all their personal information while creating their accounts. In addition to this, parents must advise their children to use only their first names for their profiles on the internet. Using only the first names ensures their security from the possible threats of identity theft in the online world.

Along with educating children, parents must be strict in allowing children to create account only when parents are added as friends. Parents can keep a check of the friends list of their children and also monitor what their child post on their page.

The parents must discourage their children to enter all the important information on social networking sites. This information includes the cell phone numbers, addresses, and various passwords. Parents must tell their children that the information that they post on internet is in the public domain and that anyone can use that information to harass them.

Scott Cantroll is computer security specialist dedicated to educating parents and computer users about computer and Internet safety and security. I have created a Web site, http://www.internetsafetycenter.com , where parents can learn more about cyberbullying, viruses, antivirus software, spyware, social networking dangers, and identity theft.

Scott Cantrell

Social Networking - Stay Connected All the Time

Many businesses and companies now use this as a medium of advertising and look at it as a channel to improve sales. You meet a friend who is a part of a community and then learn about the concept. You like it and want to be a part of it and that is how it all starts. It basically works on word of mouth.

So there is no compulsion or strings attached. It could be a home business or finance business, you decide, you enjoy the rewards and tell others about your experience. This way your group keeps growing and anybody you introduce will fall under your name. So you keep earning for many years and also get a share of their earnings.

Look at it any way; it's a win-win situation for all - business or brand, network group and individuals. You can exchange everyday talk and new ideas over the internet and in meetings. You will be working or doing business, but in a more friendly and informal way. Some people like this and also works if you are a parent of just want some additional income.

It's also a great place to make new friends and meet people who share the same feelings and thoughts as you. There are many such social websites and they include a broad range of subjects such as - age, location, hobbies, politics and passion.

When it's a busy life, staying in touch with friends is easy with online Social Networking. You get connected and stay connected to like minded people from any corner of the world.

Emmanuel Mba is an internet marketer expert for the past three years, I am most interested in affiliate marketing , article marketing and blogging. You are welcome to visit my blog at http://bisinternetmarketing.com/blog

Emmanuel Mba

Social Networking - Using Facebook and Twitter to Build Your Business As Part of the Conversation

If you are on Facebook and Twitter, you already know how many people there are and about the interactivity that is going on. But you must get involved or it will all pass you by. Become part of the conversation and you will reap the rewards. Be seen as anti-social and no one will know you exist. It is completely up to you. In many ways, social networking is like networking in your own community in the offline world. That just takes a lot longer before you see any results, whereas social networking can happen in minutes or hours.

I currently have more than 3,600 friends on Facebook. I wish them happy birthday when I see that it is their special day. This feature is on your home page, and shows up automatically each day. It only takes a few minutes to go to their profiles and write something on their wall. Many times I am the only one who does this because the person does not have many friends. Sometimes that same person joins my list later in the day. I also belong to about 30 groups and have become friends with people in these groups. I choose the groups that are of interest to me and that have people who may be interested in what I do. Then I started my own Facebook group and invited my friends to join it. I now have more seven hundred people that I can communicate with regularly through my group. There are unlimited possibilities on Facebook, but you must be sociable.

Twitter works the same way. Follow me and see how it works. I notice that many Twitterers are passive and anti-social. The result? They do not connect with others and miss out on the opportunities. I have been asked to speak at a seminar, connected with someone I wanted to interview for one of my teleseminars, and added many people to my list, all by tweeting on a regular basis. Sometimes I tell people what course I have coming up and other times I share something I am doing with my family. I am also connected to Twitter through other sites, so sometimes I tweet without even being on my computer. When I post to my blog or publish an article online, this information is automatically tweeted for me.

The social networking work is endless, so become a part of it and watch your online business grow. Think about it this way; you can become extremely sociable on the internet and you don't even have to get dressed up and leave the house.

And now I invite you to join me for free weekly teleseminars that will teach you how to write, market, and sell your articles and ebook to increase your visibility, credibility and passive income by visiting http://www.EbookWritingandMarketingSecrets.com and also learn the technology needed to run an online business.

Connie Ragen Green

Social Networking and How to Use It I

Unless you have been spending a few years up in a space station, or are a time traveler from far in the distant past, or even the future, who knows, you will have heard of social networking.

What 's that? Never heard of it? Of course you have. MySpace has more visitors than Google, and MySpace is an example of a social networking site. Yup, that 's what they are called, that and Facebook.

YouTube as well, but that 's for videos. In fact there are different flavors of social networking sites according to their specialty. MySpace is currently very popular, and is the internet equivalent of the local street corner. It 's a place where you can hang out at and chat to your mates. Except your mates can be from all over the world and of every nationality.

You join a social networking site in much the same way as you join a club. One of your mates invites you to come along, or you simple enter the site and join yourself. Once there, you let others know who you are and what you like doing by creating your profile. Since your friend asked you along, you first connect to their network, then to other networks as you get to find others with the same interests as you.

You use blogs and message boards, even instant messaging and direct internet connections to contact people you want to communicate with and talk to. VoIP telephone systems such as Skype let you speak to them free, and webcams are great for video communications. Social networking allows you to meet new friends and also to make very useful new contacts, and if used correctly could be very advantageous to you. However, each site has its own rules, and breach them at your peril!!

Do you want to learn more about how I do it? I have just completed my brand new guide to article marketing success, "Your Article Writing and Promotion Guide "

Download it free here: Internet Article Marketing

Do you want to learn how to build a massive list fast? Visit here: Email List Building

Sean Ray

Social Networking and Online Dating

You have to possess a characteristic of a matchmaker if you want to make it big in starting an online business for social networking and online dating. There are massive amounts of individuals who utilize online dating and social networking sites to look for a friend or companion than looking for someone outside. You have all the liberty to select from the characteristics and personality that is visible in the website; and that is the primary reason. Before you initialize your online business, you should devote time and perseverance to surf and learn about other social networking or online dating site so that you will have a general and advance idea about the ins and outs of online dating business.

You have to ensure before you start your dating business that you have to locate the best possible model for your business that possesses the capability and ability to give excellent service to individuals who are looking for a social network or online dates. While on the process, gather all the experts in this field while filtering out any useless elements. This will aid your customers to feel the element of security while engaging in your social networking site to look for their future partners. In the long run, if your customers are satisfied with your services, they will be the ones to recommend your online dating site to their own network of friends.

You will also need the services of an excellent website designer and online hosting group in order to jumpstart an efficient and effective social networking and online dating website. When you have these people around, it will help in enhancing your website to deliver more traffic and be on the top list in the search engines; thus, you will attract a lot of prospective customers. Meanwhile, you can also consider the fact that you can become your own host and controlling your own server to have a thorough learning of all that tackles the nature of online business.

When you start your own social networking site, you dream of a well recognized and successful website. And in order to become successful, a good informative content and publicity cost should manifest in your website. You have to be different with others in terms of impression and distinctiveness. In order to have an edge from other online dating site, you have to shell out ample amount of capital so that you can reach as many individuals as possible.

You also have to avail of the power of Search Engine Optimization and consider putting your social networking and online dating service on several search engines. This will make you boost your traffic in a productive manner.

A pinch of determination, spoonful of finances and a glass of determination will take you a long way and meet your success in this kind of business. The primary ingredients to succeed in your own online dating service are the desire to win and the skill on how to utilize dating software. You must allocate a budget for your software for this certain category of online exchange and an excellent devotion to build a winning online dating career.

http://www.datingsitebuilder.com/

Nico Kurniawan

Social Networking Basics 101 - How to Get Started Right Here Right Now

Before online businesses can begin using social networking effectively, they need to fully understand these services and why they have so much valuable potential.

History of Social Networking

Early on in the creation of the Internet, efforts were made to develop software and programs that would allow users to stay closely connected. Those efforts rarely went anywhere. In fact, one of the earliest versions of a social network was created by Classmates.com, a site that is still around and still building its user base.

The concept of the site was to provide a venue in which people who had gone to high school or college together could re-connect virtually or just check in to see what others from their schools were doing now. Today, Facebook has taken a similar concept, blended it with aspects of MySpace, and created a more popular and more user-friendly version.

Basics of Social Networking

While online business professionals want to stay in touch with leads or current customers, most people who use social networking services want something similar. The whole goal of these sites is to stay connected via communication.

Obviously, the types of communication you use will vary depending on whether you are running a business or chatting about high school couples but the overall purpose of these sites don't change.

To be successful with social networking, however, you have to know how to communicate with people through online means. For example, even on a social networking site you would never write to another person using all capital letters.

Social Networking Brings Out the Best and Removes the Dark Side of Humanity- Baloney!

Many social networking gurus believe that the Internet and all the latest social networking sites are bringing humanity together and creating connections and friends. I would say that I completely disagree, in fact, I think there is more than ample proof that social networking is bringing out the absolute worst in people and dummying down our populations. Let me explain.

Not long ago a social networking expert and I were discussing hit issue and she told me; "I believe we will never get to reach an enhanced level of society if we contently evoke the dark side of humanity."

Wow, I thought, this is a really wonderful statement and a testament to her character and attitude towards humanity. That's great what an awesome person. However, I thought, what do you say to people who point out that online anonymity and the new paradigms of social online networking is bringing out the worst innate characteristics of the species we refer to as human? I mean the argument works both ways.

Social Network type sites do a lot for self-esteem and empowering folks, unfortunately to the point of allowing them to commote, complain and carry on about anything and everything; well, is that really serving humanity? The example perhaps most given are the Internet Forums cat fights, Blogger attacks, and even the use of social media by International Terrorist groups now to recruit and get money donated to their causes. I suppose most of the Internet gurus of these latest trends are aware of this?

Social networking has made more of that possible, even promoting the mobs against the individual that the social networks have claimed to empower? Maybe the online social gurus should have given more study to the philosophy of these trends, rather than calling them a victory for the human endeavor? Do you see it differently, have you considered this, and if so, how do you negate one side of the equation for the other? Please consider this, as my article is only to make you think.

Lance Winslow - Lance Winslow's Bio . Lance Winslow is also Founder of the Detail Guys, a cool little Franchise Company; http://www.detailguys.com/founder.shtml/ .

Lance Winslow

Social Networking For HR - Driving Recruitment and Engagement

Social networks have risen to such popular heights because they satisfied a basic human need: to be connected to the rest of the world. Through social media websites, users can create virtual communities that allow them to interact with like-minded individuals from all parts of the world. Because of the effectiveness of online communities in disseminating information, social media websites have become indispensable tools in various industries. These days, human resources social networking is becoming the new trend for HR professionals. They can put the power of a social network to work in recruitment, employee engagement, increasing retention and more.

Recruiting with social media

Recruiting and brand building is social media's biggest use for human resources currently. It's not uncommon to find companies recruiting through social media such as Facebook and Twitter. HR professionals are recruiting employees using LinkedIn and applying practically the same principles that marketing and advertising use to attract a particular targeted audience.

HR can maximize the use of social networking given the right strategies. Here are a couple of tips to keep in mind.

Go to the right networks

It doesn't make sense to explore social networks that do not meet your targeted demographic. For instance, if you're in search of a person to fit a high-level position such as a product manager, it would save you time if you stayed away from MySpace or other sites known for its younger subscribers. These networks are great if you're looking to recruit summer interns, entry-level employees or even college part-time job seekers.

Recruiting employees using LinkedIn is a great idea because the site is known for having subscribers who are professionals. It is a great search venue if you're looking for experienced individuals in practically any industry.

Take the time to search

It's going to take a bit of practice to learn the ropes of human resources social networking. For starters, you want to master searching through these networks - streamlining each search to ensure that the results are trimmed down to the best candidates. You want to avoid using broad searches because they come up with far too many results that you wouldn't be able to efficiently weed out.

Move or lose!

It's also important to note that you're not the only organization or head-hunter recruiting through social media. Others have begun tapping into this technique long before you have started exploring it. So it's important that you act on a qualified candidate as soon as possible because other people are sure to have their eyes set on that potential employee as well.

Be professional

Even in cyberspace, appearances are everything. If you're going to put up a profile on Facebook or Twitter for recruiting, you want to maintain a certain degree of professionalism in your pages. It seems obvious to say it, but it's also important to be nice. Don't treat people rudely. Word of mouth works fast, especially in a diverse online community. You don't want to be the subject of a blog post or youtube video making the rounds of how you were unprofessional to a particular applicant.

Use social networks to promote employee engagement

According to studies, employee engagement can make your organization perform 2.6 times better than other companies. When employees feel passionate about the company's products and services, sales improve. Social networks can have a huge impact on employee engagement, and more and more organizations now use it to increase involvement and commitment among workers.

Using social networks, you can do all the three internal communication components of successful workforce engagement - that is, TALK, LISTEN, and RESPOND. If Web 2.0 social networking is successfully integrated into your company's culture, you can send positive team building messages instantly, communicate to all employees faster, and get feedback right away.

Many successful companies (Shell, General Electric, Procter & Gamble) use Facebook to connect networks of employees who don't have the time to interact personally every day. They don't just rely on this social network for instant messaging. More importantly, they use it to send messages espousing emotional attachment, commitment, and involvement among employees - for example, stories about the company's charitable involvements, news about career growth possibilities, and recognition of exemplary performances. Social networks have a high success rate in generating engagement.

These are just a few of the many tips that you have to keep in mind when working with social networking websites. But at the end of the day, it's still important to remember that the best way to connect with your workforce is directly and in person.

The Center for Competitive Management (CCM) provides you, today's business professional, with the information you need to stay on top of your career. CCM is dedicated to bringing you the information you need to succeed. Our products include audio conferences, training resources, research papers and more.

Want more information on this topic? http://c4cm.com/hr/socialnet.htm

We understand your work life is busier than ever, with less time available for training and education. That's why it's our goal to help you gain the knowledge you need in the most convenient methods available.

We're the one resource that gives you an insider's advantage for staying on top of the issues in your industry. CCM's content is designed to help busy professionals like you with your critical responsibilities and improve the performance of your company. With over 10 years of experience in providing up-to-the minute, high-impact information, you can count on CCM for authoritative and practical guidance - and save time and money getting it.

Center for Competitive Management http://c4cm.com/hr/index.htm

Tina Nacrelli

Social Networking On Squidoo - Review

A Soup To Nuts Approach To Socializing On Squidoo -- From Setting Up A Free Account To Maximizing The Amount Of Laser Targeted Traffic Your Modules Will Bring.

In her ebook Tiffany Dow makes simple and easy work for anyone that is looking to set up a new lens on Squidoo. A quick and easy read.

I was impressed with her no hype, no filler approach to what one needs to do and will have the reader setting up their new lens in record time without any details that could confuse or frustrate the new lensmaster.

In this book you will learn:

* How to speak the Squidoo language.

* How to launch a new lens that's meant to attract attention.

* How to aim your lens at your target audience.

* How to get a Top 100 LensRank and bump up in the SERPS.

* How to nail down your niche within Squidoo.

* Everything new about Sqidoo -- Changes that will impact your socialization strategy.

It's a quick and clear read that spans six chapters and just forty seven pages. When finished you'll know exactly what to do and how to do it.

In addition, for those that may be learning challenged, she has thrown in a step by step video that is sure to remove any mystery or confusion.

She also throws in The Multi-Layered Mindset Of Web 2.0 as a bonus. She says, "It's not a buzzword or mysterious new advertising tactic - It's about raising your strategic planning to a level that matches the evolution of the World Wide Web".

Web 2.0 is another evolution of the Internet and it's all about the people. A must read!

All in all I found Tiffany's Ebook "Social Networking On Squidoo" to be an informative and useful approach for anyone that wants to broaden their marketing strategies, making common sense use of the Social Networking site known as "Squidoo"

Hey There Future LensMaster, Better hurry - because right now, someone could be stealing your prime keywords and phrases! http://newspub.blogspot.pk/

Art Luff

Social Networking is Relationship Building - Tips From a Serial Networker!

Sales managers everywhere emphasize the importance of getting referrals after the sale. They will argue that if you have laid the proper foundation during your sales presentation, you can even get referrals from people who did not buy from you. They are right, to a point. Customers are increasingly hesitant to give referrals to people they barely know for a service that has yet to be provided. And how many sales professionals do you know that always interact with their customer after services have been rendered?

It makes sense then to try building a more predictable referral stream by networking with influencers in an industry similar to yours. You typically meet these people at Chamber of Commerce events, hard-contact networking meetings and now more than ever, online. Linkedin, Facebook, Twitter, Ning, Plaxo, the list goes on an on of different sites that can facilitate relationship building. Fortunately, some of the principles for being successful networking offline are the same for networking online!

Principle #1: Thou shall stick with it!

The Nielson Company recently released a report that only 30 percent of the people who sign up for Twitter use it after their first month with the service. Successful BNI members know that many people give up after the first few meetings. The currency of networking is trust, and trust takes time to build. If you give it an adult time frame of at least three months, you are much more likely to see the results you are looking for.

Principle #2: Thou shall pick wisely!

Not all offline networking groups are created equal! Some chambers of commerce are heavily dependent on retail clients, others have several members from Fortune 1000 companies. Trade associations are more active than others. Strong contact networking groups are all individual because they reflect the personalities of the members. Being choosy upfront gives you better odds of accomplishing your goals.

Luckily, most online networking options do not require an up-front charge. This allows you to look at several and determine which is right for you. One method that works well is looking at your top clients and finding out which services they use. One distinct advantage of this method is that they are more likely to publicly endorse you, lending you their credibility with their network. This can be a useful jump start to your online networking efforts.

Principle #3: Thou shall participate!

Offline, the options are well documented. You can serve on the leadership team of your BNI chapter, stand in as an ambassador of your chamber or help in the planning of your trade association convention. All of these actions make you more visible and give people a compelling reason to talk with you.

Online options are just as plentiful. With Twitter, make sure you tweet everyday. On Linkedin, answer questions. On Biznik, post articles for your business. On Slideshare, comment on other presentations. The key is to participate on a regular basis so people can get to know you.

Principle #4: Thou shall respect my space!

Both online and offline, you need to respect the boundaries of your networking partners. That means not poaching customers, being clear on what you bring to the table and responding to your networking partners in the ways they expect. Online networking presents its own unique challenges, however. Specifically, when someone has a wall that they allow you to post things on. Facebook is the most clear example. That wall belongs to them and should not be cluttered with your billboard message. Think of it as someone switching the sign on your business to theirs because you get more traffic. An absolute no-no both online and off!

Principle #5: Thou shall always follow through!

When you do start to receive referrals, it is critical that you follow through on them immediately. Anything less risks your ability to close business and hurts the credibility of the person giving you the referral. There are few surefire ways to make certain you will earn more referrals, and this is one of them!

At the heart of all networking efforts is relationships. Your ability to build relationships, healthy and sustainable relationships, will determine your ability to build a solid pipeline of referrals. The effort you put into being your authentic self online and offline will be paid back in the form of strong referral sources!

Part-time blogger and full-time networker, David Lingholm is the leadoff hitter for Basso Design Group http://www.bassodesigngroup.com He ensures clients have a strong brand image with excellent web design properly communicated through social media, search engine marketing and search engine optimization.

Lingholm developed a real passion for helping people build their business through referrals while working as a director for BNI of Michigan, supporting chapters in metropolitan Detroit. This passion drives him to continue advocating that business owners and sales professionals make networking a significant part of their marketing plans, a topic he continues to write and speak about. It also has led him to become an area connector for Motor City Connect. When his head is not buried in a book, he serves of the Board of Trustees for the First Unitarian Universalist Church of Detroit, the Maple Valley Memorial Scholarship Foundation and Operation: Kid Equip, getting kids in Oakland County, MI the school supplies they need so they can focus on learning. If all else fails, you might even find him whitewater rafting in West Virginia or anywhere else the water is wild!

David Lingholm

Social Networking Sites Can Generate Money

Many articles have already been written about how a person with an account in a social networking site can make money. We'd love to share that, too, but what we really want you to know is that, as an owner of a social networking site, you can generate money other than from account upgrades of your members.

Here are three things that will bring in some money for you if you own a social networking site.

Affiliate marketing Surely, you have heard about it. It's a form of free advertising. Here's how it works. There's a website that wants advertising space in your social networking site or dating site. Instead of an outright payment for an ad which may or may not work, you get paid a portion of a transaction that the advertiser closed with a customer who visited his site by visiting the ad on your site. It's a referral system that does not even require you to put in work.

Vice-versa, you can also be the advertiser and look for an affiliate who can lend you advertising space. You'll pay him a portion of a transaction he 'referred' to you, as well.

Google Ads Google ads are text or image ads that appear at a relevant website. If a website talks about tennis, tennis ads will appear at different locations on the page. If a website talks about jewelry, jewelry ads will appear. Therefore, at a dating site or social networking site such as yours, signing up for Google ads will generate dating ads and any related ads on your site. You get to be paid every time a visitor gos on an ad.

Member-centric developments Any website, no matter how great, will always have some room for improvement. Ask for your members' feedback and make changes in the functionality or navigation of your site so that it becomes easier for them to use your dating site or social networking site. By keeping your members happy, they will only be glad to include your link to their email signatures and talk about you to other people. By making sure the ones who already signed up with you are always satisfied, your business could keep growing even if you haven't even launched maximum efforts to get the word out about your social media or dating business.

http://www.datingsitebuilder.com/

Nico Kurniawan

Social Networking Sites Can Help You Find a Job

Are You New to Social Networking?

Did you know that you can use social networking sites such as Facebook and Twitter to help you find a job? In fact, Nielson Online, a marketing research company, reports that over two-thirds of the global online community uses social networking sites. Many of these people are using such sites to contact employers and share tips with other job seekers. So, which are the best networking sites to help you? Check out the following to find out which sites are most popular among laid off job seekers.

Employers are Looking for You on Facebook

A few years ago Facebook was used by college students to make friends and post embarrassing pictures of each other. Now, however, Facebook is used by people of all ages, and more and more employers are using this site to recruit workers. Facebook has a "marketplace" feature where you can search for jobs and email potential employers of your interest. You can also join common interest groups, find people in your area or with similar problems, and swap tips with them. Facebook is a great way for the laid off worker to network. You can find old friends or co-workers and ask them if they've heard of any job openings. You can search for people by using their email and once you've added enough friends, Facebook can suggest people you know by searching through its network. Facebook is easy to use and it's free to start an account.

Twitter Popularity is Growing Among Laid Off Job Seekers

Twitter is similar to blogging and you'll be expected to update your status with "tweets" fairly often. You can update either via the website or through mobile phone texting. You can also link your Twitter account to your Facebook account, so all your Facebook friends can see your updates. Laid off workers have been turning to Twitter in droves and the site recently started its own job search engine at twitterjob-search.com, where you can find discussion boards for specific industries. If you decide to use Twitter make sure you keep your profile professional and include what job you are looking for. You'll also want to Twitter about things relevant to your industry. If you have an area of expertise, give advice and help others. The idea is to grow your network, ask for advice, and for referrals.

LinkedIn is Used by Laid Off Professionals

Unlike Twitter and Facebook, LinkedIn is geared toward career networking and is considered by many as the top networking site for job seekers. LinkedIn is commonly used by industry professionals, marketers, salespeople, and now increasingly by laid off job seekers. The strategy with LinkedIn is similar to that of the other sites. You'll want to create a professional profile, participate in groups, and grow your network.

Social Networking Sites Could Help You

So if you were part of a mass layoff or just an individual who may have been singled out,social networking is vitally important to your future success. Social networking sites have really taken off in the past few years and it now outranks email in popularity. Given the economic downturn, more and more laid off employees are searching for their next job by using online networks. So, whether it's Facebook, Twitter, LinkedIn or the many other networking sites out there, social networking could be what lands you your next job.

Was this article helpful? Would you like to learn how to cope with layoffs and unemployment? Visit my site, will work for food , and find more interesting articles and tips!

Jim A Landis

Social Networking Sites For Business in Six Easy Steps

Social Networking Sites have increasingly been used for business purposes these days. Social Networking in general has become immensely popular over the last couple of years. In fact, if you go to Alexa.com and look up the top 10 or the top 100 sites on the internet in terms of traffic, many of those will be social networking sites. These sites, while they are a great way to socialize, connect with old friends, and meet new people, can also be very effective at generating new business for your Network Marketing or Internet marketing business. Here are a couple of steps on how to properly set-up and utilizing Social Networking for business.

Step #1) On every social networking site, the first thing that you want to do is to register and set up something known as a profile. Here is the best way to set-up your profile. Tell a little story about yourself, and how it relates to you in network marketing or your business. You absolutely want to include is a link to your capture page or whatever web site you want to promote on there.

Here is a little hint for your profile, if you are in network marketing or using this social networking site for business, don't make your profile something like "My business is the best business and you would be a fool not to join it". That is a HUGE turn-off to people and no one will listen to you. Put something relevant about yourself.

Step #2) Do a search for groups on that site where people in your industry or target market might be located or have joined. If you are in Internet Network Marketing, go ahead and do a search for "groups" that are related to MLM or Network Marketing or Home Business or Internet Marketing. This is known as your target market.

Step #3) Join as many of those groups on that Social Networking site as you possibly can, the more the better. Remember these are social networking sites, right? By virtue of you belonging to a group on there, people will naturally want to become what is known as "friend" or "contact" with you.

Step #4) If someone invites you to be their friend, never disapprove that friendship. Always accept it. Even it looks like someone you might not want to do business with; you never know where that contact might lead. When you do accept that friendship, go ahead and send a brief message back to that person thanking them for requesting your friendship and maybe ask them what they are doing on that particular site. Some people are there for fun, some for business. Get to know those people a little bit, network with them, that is the nature of using social networking sites for business.

Step #5) Go out and look for a few people who might be there to network and invite them as a friend. The key is to network with them, and add value to your relationship with them, and you will find that what you give, you will get back tenfold.

Step #6) Always include a link to your lead capture page on your message you send back and forth to them. Don't ever advertise your MLM or opportunity or whatever, get to know people and all you do is just include your link to your lead capture page with your free offer in your signature block.

If you don't overtly advertise and spam people, you will find that they will go on the link you are including in your correspondence with them. Otherwise, you will find that these sites create little value for social networking for business.

Each Social Networking site has little nuances to it, and you will need to tweak your techniques on each site you go to. Remember that the key here is to never spam people, and to truly build relationships with these people and you will find that you can very quickly social networking sites for business an essential part of your overall business strategy.

Kurt Henninger is a successful Network marketer helping average people to have extraordinary success with their online business ventures. SuccessfulNetworkMarketingNow.com

Kurt Henninger

Social Networking Skills - Are We Becoming Socially Inept?

Although social marketing and networking isn't new it seems to be all the rage these days. Networking is about building relationships but have we forgotten the art of socializing? We're all born natural networkers because we're hard wired to be social. I guess you could say we're "pack animals". Unlike the animal kingdom we have cognitive abilities, we can look at a situation and determine the best way to proceed.

Building a network marketing business or any type of business relies on the strength of relationships whether it's customers or business partners. As children we are especially social. Kids will meet some one and decide pretty quickly if they want to be friends. They have no real agenda other than some basic expectations and to make new friends.

Fast forward into adulthood. Things can get complicated because of the perceptions we've accumulated over the years. Different lessons learned, some from personal experience and some taught to us by family, friends and our peers. What's interesting about networking online is many people act differently online than they do in the "real world". If you're in a business your goal in social marketing is to introduce your business or products to other people.

How many times has some one contacted you within a social networking site, barely introduced themselves and then gave you the sales pitch? Sometimes it feels like being invited out to dinner and then being told you have to pay the bill! Where's the relationship? Where's the know, like and trust? Relationships take time. Unfortunately we live in a society of instant gratification. We want our food fast. We don't want to wait in any line. We want our success to happen overnight. We want everything done yesterday.

Relationships never worked like that and never will. If you want changes in your life to last for the long term, be it business or personal it takes time and it has to be done right. Think about the time and effort you take to get to know some one when you meet them face to face. Think about how you feel when some one else take the time and effort to get to know you. Socializing online is no different. You are a real person connecting with real people.

Janet Napora lives in Northeast Pennsylvania. She is a network marketer and personal development advocate. She provides tips and training at http://JanetNapora.com

Janet Napora

Social Networking Tips - Using Online Services to Build a Sense of Community - Part I

As the age of technology has progressed, millions of users have migrated to the use of social networking sites such as Myspace, Facebook, and Twitter. Social networking sites are defined as web-based services that allow individuals to construct a profile that is available to the public or that can be viewed by a selective few. Members of the site are also able to communicate with other members who they share or wish to share a connection with. It also allows members to view and share their friends and connections with others as well give them the same capability. Social networking is unique because not only does it allow people to meet and interact with strangers but it allows members to socialize and show off their own social network and status.

Although many social networking sites have different features, the majority of the sites have a personal profile feature that lists friends that are also members of the site. Members are able to list information that introduces themselves to other members. The member is asked questions to describe themselves such as age, location, interests, and a section usually entitled "About Me". Members are also encouraged to customize their profiles by uploading photos, graphics, and media to suit the preferences.

Members are usually able to choose who can view their profiles. Not all social networking sites have privacy features. Some make profiles visible to anyone who has a paid account. MySpace users have the option of making their profiles open to the public or limiting access to those they choose as friends. Facebook is different, as members become part of the same network and then have access to profiles in that particular network unless they are denied permission. Twitter on the other hand, is accessed by followers who send "tweets" to the members asking "What are you doing?" to find up what others are up to.

Dave Hale, Ph.D., has twenty-three years' experience in design and delivery of training programs for public, private, government and non-profit centers. Dave is the CEO of DHI-Communications, an international business coaching and training consultancy, specializing in Web 2.0 business development and marketing. Dave is widely regarded as one of the top business coaches for Web 2.0 Entrepreneurs.

Dave is the author of The High Performance Entrepreneur: 12 Essential Strategies to Supercharge Your Startup Business. David's work and books have been featured on national television, radio, and print media. To obtain more information on how to make barrels of cash in business and instantly receive my FREE CD and Business Journal go to http://www.DrDaveHaleOnline.com and http://www.buyhiperbusinessmomentum.com

David Hale

Social Networking Websites - Your Connection to Online Communications & Relationships

Social networking websites are a phenomenon on the Internet today. They allow members to express themselves, share interests, connect with old friends and make new ones. No longer just for teenagers or college students, people of all ages and backgrounds have discovered that they can enhance their lives and promote their businesses in any number of ways through the connections they make at social networking websites. Business owners are provided with new opportunities to network, sell products and services, while organizations can get their important messages across or request donations. Some social networking sites offer and actively promote business profiles.

Besides establishing important social and business relationships, social networking members can join groups and forums to communicate easily on any number of topics important to them. But, the whole experience really starts with the personal or business profile page. That's where members can truly and uniquely express themselves by designing a page that reflects their personality or the message they're trying to deliver.

Some social networking websites really go out of their way to provide the best tools so that members can build imaginative and customizable profiles to enhance their networking experience and, of course, to keep members coming back.

When building your personal or business profile page, you can post background and contact information as well as up-to-date messages. Blogs and Forums provide additional ways for members to express themselves; they can access other member's journals and post their own comments. Linkbacks on business profiles help promote a company's main website.

The experience of building and adding to a personal profile on social media websites can be so satisfying that some people spend more time at their computers than they do in any other activity.

Ginger Marin is a former news writer and freelancer providing content for http://www.cybersoupcafe.com

Ginger Marin

Social Networking Websites and Job Search - Solving the Puzzle

The entire world is chanting about online social networking. Suddenly, 'networking' is gaining prominence in every field, including job search. Social and professional networking websites are mushrooming, the prominent ones being Facebook, Orkut, twitter, MySpace, Linkedin and others.

I understand the power of networking. And almost everybody is preaching it too. However, what concerns me more is how to harness this power of networking successfully and achieve the desired results effectively. Just spending hours online, enrolling in social networking websites, making friends and joining communities would not help. It actually requires much more time, patience and tact.

The key is to do this tactfully and subtly. It is not a one time work. You are jobless right now, you need a job, you go online and enroll yourself in a number of social as well as professional networking websites, create a profile and start asking for any job openings. Hardly anybody is going to respond to you!

What one needs to realize is that it is 'networking' and networking takes time! You need to build it slowly and steadily. You can not build a well when you're thirsty! Similarly, you just can't expect effective results instantly with networking websites.

So, how do you go about it? The most important point is - do not wait till the last hour to join the social networking websites! Join in this very minute. The earlier you join and the longer you have been around in the networking websites, the better. Make friends and join communities that interest you, where you can be active. Remember that its not just size of the network, but the level of interaction within the network that matters.

So ensure that you take part in it actively. Exchange notes, update about events which you might think may benefit the group, ask questions and help others with their queries... when you need help, these same people would be the ones providing it!

It is also very important to maintain the right balance between your social and professional communications. Social networking websites are much more than just search engines. You keep in touch with your friends, family and colleagues. You share your personal life with them. If you are not doing so and are strictly using it for your professional needs, it would not work. At the same time, if you are maintaining only social contacts and are not leveraging the networking website for your professional requirements, the entire idea is nullified. Hence, it is important to maintain a correct balance of both. The bad news is that there is no equation or formula for this. It's all about trial and errors and your personal instincts.

Also remember that social and professional networking websites are not a substitute to the personal offline networking. You will still need to make calls, meet people personally and maintain that human touch. The edge these online networking websites gives you is that it is available 24 hours and enables you to keep in touch from anywhere. It compliments your personal networking skills.

This article is written by Prashant Parikh, Founder CEO, http://www.faayda.com/ , an integrated job search website in India, to provide valuable insight and guidance for networking and job search. Prashant is an expert in the recruitment industry especially online job search techniques and offers useful insights on the same. To read more of his interviews and to know more go to http://blog.faayda.com/

Prashant Parikh

Social Networking, Football Style

All football fans want their opinion heard, whether its serious blogging or just telling your workmate that a goal should have been given offside. Its everyday chat and the lifeblood of millions of people in hundreds of countries.

Social Media is growing apace and with it websites and forums on all subjects where you can converse with people of similar interest. Football has such a huge appeal that there are thousands of sites already up which allow discussion of your favourite teams and the latest action. Many of these sites focus on particular clubs so that the focus is directed at the latest goings on at the club, who is playing that is not good enough, who they should buy next, how terrible the referee was in the last match etc. Unfortunately some of these sites often attract people that think it is clever to swear and name call within their posts so look for a site that is well moderated if you decide to join the fray.

As a fan of a particular club I do tend to visit a few of the sites for my team and read the latest opinions but in general I like to participate in more open discussion so I go to a site that is less focused mostly. If you can find a site with blogs , videos, opinions polls, forums etc it becomes fun and you can become part of the community very easily or even import your own community. Its possible now to bring in your own set of fans for a particular club and set up your own group within a bigger site. If you are a local club without a website you can form your own community within these sites now with your own unique forum and club page set up in minutes. Your club members can build personal pages and even load videos or pictures of the latest match. If your club has communication problems like posting the team for the match at the weekend its absolutely ideal.

I use http://www.thebackofthenet.com but as it has all these facilities and more but there are choices out there that could benefit your club without spending any money. These sites are fun and free to everybody that is interested in football. The content is all contributed by members who are football lovers from around the world and it changes everyday so its a great place to visit. I hope you will go and get involved if you love football.

Chris Archer has been a follower and participant in football for many years. He has forthright views on football and loves to share them. He likes to discuss professional and local football on the social media site http://www.thebackofthenet.com

Chris J Archer

Social Networking, Negative Attitudes and Business Change Management

Web 2.0 social networking sites such as Twitter, LinkedIn, and Facebook can be extraordinarily useful tools in the current business climate. They can be used to keep business associates in the loop about current happenings in real time. They provide a venue to connect with potential clients, polish a digital rolodex, and exchange ideas. LinkedIn provides forum space for this last purpose. For the change facilitator, this can be a golden opportunity to compare notes with others involved in the business change profession.

One big advantage of forums is that they can serve as sounding boards to prevent the development of tunnel vision. It can be easy to get locked into one modality regarding business change, but sound criticism from other business change facilitators can expose unknown weaknesses. Unfortunately, with the advantages that social networking sites offer come the inevitable disadvantages. Forums can easily turn into gripe sessions that can effect or represent biases in the work environment.

A common complaint among professionals is that managers get in the way of the process. When this attitude is perpetuated in social networking it can bleed into the change facilitator's interaction with their client. This creates a hostile working relationship that is less likely to produce a successful business change.

Like any generalization, the idea that managers get in the way does not stand up to evaluation. There will be the occasional manager that is opposed to the change process and works to derail it. These managers should not be considered representative. A change facilitator would not have been brought into the picture if the client was not serious about the process. Management has more than one concern when it comes to the business change process.

They are required to consider the creation of a successful change and keeping the business moving. Change projects tend to be disruptive and can be time consuming affairs, but customers must still be provided with services or products. Managers must balance the needs of both the business change and the business at hand. While they may appear to be obstructing the process, it is important for the change professional to bear in mind the conflicting needs managers are handling during the process.

For more information, please see the website: Business Change Management .

Jacob Long

Social Networking, The Pros and Cons of Social Networks

Social Networking has become increasingly popular nowadays as there are a lot of sites that offer this service. MySpace and Friendster are two of the most popular sites that aim to build communities of people who share common interests and activities, or who are interested in exploring the interests and activities of others.

THE PROS

A social networking site is like a virtual meeting place where people can hang out and discuss different topics. Anything under the sun, in fact. Some use these networking sites to promote their blogs, to post bulletins and updates or to use them as a bridge to a future love interest.

These are just a few of the reasons why social networking is getting a lot of attention lately -- it makes life more exciting for many people.

THE CONS

However, it would be best to make sure that safety and security are the topmost concerns of the social networking site that you currently use. This is because social networking sites require or give you the option to provide personal information such as your name, location, and email address. Unfortunately some people can take this as an opportunity for identity theft. They can copy your information and pretend to be "you" when engaging in illegal activities. Bad news! So be cautious with what you enter into an online networking site.

You could fall into the trap of someone who pretends to be somebody else. For example, they might offer you a job or want to meet up with you just to get your money. This can lead to cyberstalking, where the stalker uses electronic media such as the Internet to pursue or harass you.

THE CONCLUSION

So take your time and be careful in choosing who to trust so you can hopefully avoid this sort of unpleasant thing happening to you. Apart from that, social networking is great thing.

If you found this article helpful, you might appreciate my FREE report called " GET TO THE MONEY FASTER ". Get it now at http://eprofitnews.org

Article by Gary Harvey of http://FindHotMarkets.com the Internet's BIGGEST LIST of ways to find hot niches, best selling products and hot markets .

Gary Harvey

Social-Networking Sites MySpace and Facebook - It's Time For Some Change

In the last several months, there has been a lot of debate and discussion regarding the on-going policy of social-networking sites MySpace and Facebook, whereby images of mothers breastfeeding their child is removed from the users' pages under the context that it violates the sites Terms of Service against posting "pornographic" or "obscene" content. However, there's another interesting, long-term issue that this debate has brought to light regarding these types of internet sites and that is is how should we define the balance between how end users of a social-networking site communicate and share and the rights/responsibilities of the owners/managers of these online community websites. As it's pretty much understood why people are users/members of these social-networking websites, I'll start by looking at the situation from the perspective of the companies/organizations that own these Web 2.0 ventures.

For starters, there can be little doubt that as the owners/managers of these online community sites, it is their prerogative to decide not only what content they will allow to be shared on their site, but also the type of users they'll grant access to. These guidelines or rules, often described in the site's Terms of Service agreement, are meant to serve as a filter to help the site owner's build the online community they hope to attract and nurture on their domain. However, as much as these rules or regulations are meant to define the nature and makeup of the site's membership, the ultimate goal with social-networking sites is to make it as accessible and inviting to as many users as possible, thereby encouraging a heterogeneity of users to their site for interaction and communication.

Now, there's no question that both Facebook and MySpace are not considered 'specialty' sites or social-networking sites that cater exclusively to people who share a common cultural norms system or values/belief structure. And yet, reading many of the statements released by Facebook and MySpace concerning their policy of removing any images of mothers breastfeeding their babies from their respective sites, it becomes clear that there are in fact cultural norms being used to determine what kinds of interaction and sharing will be allowed on these sites, norms that not only are out of sync with most of the world, but ones that are not aligned with most state/provincial and federal laws concerning public breastfeeding. As such, it becomes a little more difficult to view these two social-networking sites as not being ones that cater more to the North-American societal segment that would agree that women can reveal portions of the breast for titillation and not because they are providing sustenance to their child.

In the 'real world', any social interaction between people is affected by the cultural/social norms of the society that they are a part of and as these 'real world' interactions are often limited by geographical proximity, there is a strong likelihood that both parties have a large number of these norms/values in common. With the creation of the internet though, people can now interact with others over wide distances, and cultural/social differences that are normally apparent in the 'real world' are less obvious. However, that doesn't mean those differences aren't there or that they don't factor into how people communicate over the internet. While this divergence in cultural/social norms may have been less apparent a few years ago when these social-networking sites were still emergent 'technologies', given the greater sense of comfort and ease end users have using these sites, it is very likely that the debate over the appropriateness of breastfeeding images on social-networking sites is but the tip of the iceberg.

While Facebook and MySpace have been successful to date in creating a vibrant, diverse membership, the fact that these sites deem something to be "offensive" which the majority of the world's cultures and societies see as being perfectly natural indicates a need for re-evaluation of how their sites function. Perhaps instead of one generic site, geographic-regional ones will need to be created that better relate and mirror the norms and cultural standards of people in various parts of the world so that members of these online communities won't be subjected to having their exchange of information and ideas being regulated on the basis of one specific region's social/cultural norms. At the moment, MySpace is in fact currently testing out over 20 different country-specific beta versions of their site, though perhaps this is more a result of losing ground to Facebook in 2008 among international users of these social-networking sites than a recognition that a more broad understanding of social mores and values is needed for such sites to be relevant outside of their geographic physical base.

Regardless, the debate over the removal of pictures of breastfeeding moms from these two social-networking sites has highlighted the reality that these kinds of online community sites have to adapt new measures to ensure that they not only retain their global presence on the internet, but also so that they remain relevant to as many internet users by not restricting their interpretation of acceptable conduct to a narrow cultural viewpoint as it currently does.

You can read more of Tanveer's writings at his personal blog site, "So, what were we talking about again?" at http://tanveernaseer.wordpress.com/

Tanveer Naseer

Stand Out in Networking Circles By Becoming a Subject Matter Expert

Over time, you will meet a lot of people through your networking activities. It can be a challenge for you to stand out and for people to remember you.

Pick a topic on which you have some knowledge to share. It should be something you enjoy keeping up with on a regular basis. It doesn 't matter if this subject relates to your career or your personal life.

As long as you have a passion for this topic, people will want to listen. As a result, you may become a resource for others on this topic, which is very important for making networking effective.

Create a Web Site

As you gather information on your subject matter, an efficient way to organize everything is by creating a Web site. With a Web site, you can provide several resources in one place.

When you meet people, you can direct them to this Web site. Sharing information with others is very important in networking.

It 's important for this site to be separate from your company 's Web site. By developing a standalone site, you will be able to keep this as your own no matter where you work.

Part of networking is branding yourself. Take the time to put together a useful Web site that you can share with others. For example, I have created a business and networking resources Web site at http://www.jacobsohn.com.

With this Web site, I have branded myself as a subject matter expert on business networking. No matter where I work, I will always be able to share this information with people.

Create an Electronic Newsletter

Another great way to brand yourself as a subject matter expert is to create and distribute an electronic newsletter. Your newsletter should include information about your expertise such as articles, resources and tips.

Whenever you meet people, you can share your newsletter with them. Make sure to get their permission before you sign people up. You want interested people to receive your newsletter.

It 's OK to include some of your work information ; such as your products or services ; in your newsletter. However, make sure you do so as a soft sell. Include it near the bottom of your newsletter.

The main goal with any newsletter should be to provide some valuable information. After people have read your newsletter for some time, they will begin to perceive you as a trusted source on your topic.

Once this happens, they may want to purchase a product or service from you. If you have the drive and ability, send your newsletter on a regular basis so you are fresh in their minds. Also, if you have a Web site, allow people to sign up for the newsletter on the site.

Write Articles

If you truly are a subject matter expert, you should have no problem writing articles about your topic. In fact, articles are an excellent way for you to express your own thoughts about a particular topic.

While it 's one thing to read articles from other people, it 's quite another to write your own. Self-expression is so important and putting your thoughts down on paper is a great way to share your expertise with others.

Find an avenue that will allow you to submit articles on a regular basis. This will allow you to stay fresh and will require you to come up with an abundance of articles. Do some research and look for a source that could use your topical knowledge such as a newspaper, magazine or an online publication.

Be proactive, approach one of these sources and persuade them that your topic would be of interest to their readers. If you convince them to let you become a columnist, you will get some great exposure. This will help you to develop your own brand.

Another important reason to write articles is because you will be able to share these with your network. Any time you can find valuable information, take the time to share this with your network.

Speak at Events

As you become a subject matter expert, people will start to take notice. In fact, you may be asked to speak at networking or business events.

It is a great honor to be selected as a speaker. Take advantage of these opportunities. Speaking is a very visible activity and you will be perceived as an expert by an array of people.

One of the nice ideas about speaking is that you can usually dictate what you will talk about and how you want to share this information with your audience. For example, you may put together an interactive presentation that will allow your participants to meet and learn from each other.

At the same time, you may want to produce your own event at which you will be the featured speaker. While you will be able to invite your network to your talk, you will be able to market the event to your local business community. This is great publicity.

Final Thought

Remember that branding yourself as an expert is very important in networking. Make yourself stand out by picking a topic of passion and sharing resources and information with others.

Without setting yourself apart, you can get lost in the mix with all the other people you will meet in networking. Be proactive, creative and have some fun.

Jason Jacobsohn is a seasoned networker who believes in relationship building as a key component to business success. He enjoys helping others succeed by making introductions, planning events, and sharing resources. In addition, Jacobsohn enthusiastically shares resources with his network through his e-mail newsletter, Network Your Way to Success, □ and http://www.jacobsohn.com , a comprehensive business and networking resources Web site. Further, he shares an additional perspective through his blog at http://www.networkinginsight.com

Jason Jacobsohn

Strategic Networking: Take the Shortest Path to Success

Do you use Ryze or LinkedIn to promote your web based business? If so, you may have noticed that everything is linked to everything else. Here's how to take the shortest path to networking success: use keywords and a targeted linking strategy.

On Ryze and other major networks, connections are happening everywhere. It's like real life, but far more obvious because it's in print before your eyes. But what you may not have noticed, is that keywords are the very thing that drives your online business connections.

Online networks such as Ryze have live links built into them for a reason. They're your opportunity to directly connect with people who can help you achieve your business goals. Such links enable you to "trace a path" from connection to connection. If you think about this long enough, it may occur to you that you can shorten that path to the best connections if you incorporate a linking strategy into your networking plan. How to go about this? Use keywords and "key people" who can help you get to the place in life where you want to be.

Include Keywords In Your Personal Profile

As you build your personal Ryze page, you'll notice that you get to add descriptive words to your profile to define who you are. You're free to use any words you want, but the idea, again, is to take the most direct route to success. So choose words, or keywords if you will, that will help you "find and be found."

Let's use your location as an example. If you go right on the state where you live, you can "pivot" on the word to see a list of every Ryze member who lives in that state, too. The same goes for every other live link you get on Ryze. You are in control of these links.

Now suppose you want to link up to people who share your personal hobbies and interests. Type in the words to describe your interests as they're most commonly known.

Let's say you're a golfer. You can attract other golf enthusiasts with the simple keyword "golf." You can of course type in something like "putting around" but what other golfer is going to choose those exact words for his interest list? Maybe one other guy, and if you can find him then you're soulmates and should probably marry each other. Just kidding!

Remember, the point of online network links is not to be original, but to make connections. If you feeling like getting creative, you can always do that on your homepage. Write fabulous copy. Include breath-taking photos. Just make sure that your links are beefed up with common keywords for prime networking opportunities.

Adding Key People: Target Your Links!

In much the same way that a smart advertiser pulls in his audience using keywords and highly targeted copy in every ad he writes, you should be pointing all your Ryze links to the people, groups, and opportunities that will point your business in a highly focused and profitable direction.

Some Ryze members try to really work the Friends List angle. Every once in a while an aggressive Ryzer sends me a message like, "Hi Dina, I noticed you didn't say hello when you stopped by my page." And then they want to add me to their Friends list right away.

First of all, I know for a fact that I never Ryzed by Joe Bagadonuts's Ryze page, and he's not going to trick me into thinking I did. So tone it down, Joe, you're coming on too strong.

Second of all, I have my own theory about Ryze, and it's that adding everyone to my Friends List is going to defeat the purpose of me being there in the first place.

Think about this: What if you could add every Ryze member to your Friend's List? Pretty cool, huh? You'd be royally hooked up with awesome connections! Right?

No. You'd be right back where you started on Ryze. A massive pool of connections to pore through to do some decent business, and you don't know where to start. Kinda paradoxical, isn't it.

The answer, of course, is to be more selective in who you link to. Hook up with those who offer services, information, support and advice that you need to grow your business. How to do this? Join networks.

Joining the Right Networks Will Bring Hits to Your Page

When you first join Ryze, join networks. Not necessarily a ton of networks, but the ones that will help forward your business objective along. This is how you get "hits" to your page. Why? Because online networks are simply a miniature model of the World Wide Web! You must get out there in order for people to see you, and you must communicate who you are and what you stand for... or no one will know you exist.

Suppose you sell all-natural coffee, and you want to do some writing for the coffee industry as well as put out a newsletter to your email subscriber list of coffee drinkers, which you don't have yet because you only just started your business. Also, somewhere down the line maybe you'd like to revamp your website, but that's not in the budget right now.

Your networking strategy whould be as follows: join a network of coffee fans, another network of natural foodies, a writing group, an email and/or ezine publishing group, and a web design group. Participate in each of those groups. Jump right into the conversation.

You'll find that networks which coincide with your Big Plan, are appealing because members are often interested in achieving the same goals as you are. In talking with them over time, you'll develop mutually beneficial relationships that lead to new opportunities.

Another perk of joining the right networks: new Ryzers and Floating Ryzers who "Ryze on by" the networks will scan the list of members, see your name, and maybe reach out to make a connection with you. That's how to be "found" by the right people. "Target" your networking, and carve a path to success and prosperity for your home-based web business.

Your Friends List is Your Circle of Trust

So now you're probably wondering what the heck that Friends List is for. Your Friends can be anybody you wish, but ideally they should be people you know and trust.

My Friends list orginates from the first dot-com group that I worked for, whose members all belonged to Ryze and urged me to join.

It also includes people I "pulled in" from the outside world. In my opinion, and if you don't agree with this, that's perfectly okay... your Ryze Friends List should be a cluster of "set connections" - your Circle of Trust. It should consist of the people with whom you've had positive prior experiences, are making current plans with, and have established solid, long-term relationships.

Why should this matter? Well, I don't know about you but I'd much rather deal with people who I KNOW AND TRUST than random others who merely added me to their friend list to build a huge following. Me, I want strong links in my people chain. But that's just me.

Example: suppose I'm looking to hire a tech guy. Will I contact a tech guy that's connected to a person I barely know? Of course not! I'll choose someone who comes with a recommendation from a trusted friend: someone on my Friends List. All the more reason to keep your Ryze Friends List "pure." I can't explain it any better than this.

Of course, not every network you join will be related to your business. You can join for the social aspect alone, and that's perfectly okay. Because another cool thing about online networking is that you can keep your groups separate if you want!

The best online networks, like Ryze, are ingeniously designed to make the most of your connections in every facet of your business and your life. In much the same way we make real-time connections, online networks afford opportunities to build profitable and trusting relationships. Why not use that to your advantage?

Liked this article? Have more of the same emailed to your inbox each month. Sign up for the Copywriting and Marketing Ezine from Dina at Wordfeeder.com and learn to write search engine friendly web copy and market your web based business for free.

Dina Giolitto

Structured Networking is Far More Effective Than Traditional Networking

Structured networking, a form of team marketing where you market through powerful, proactive referral partners is a multiplicative model, while traditional networking is a linear model. They are complementary not exclusive.

Traditional Networking Traditional networking is a style of networking where you market yourself by allowing others to get to know you. It is a linear model. You meet others one at a time, qualify them, and follow up if there is interest in your product or service.

We are all familiar with traditional networking. It is the type of networking we do at a chamber mixer or other business event. It is a soft sell approach to marketing and an effective way of meeting other business professionals who could be of help in achieving your business goals. It is an inexpensive form of marketing that allows you to meet a large number of people in a short period of time at mixers or other events.

Assuming there are opportunities for repetitive exposures to those with whom you would like to build relationships, traditional networking also creates the opportunity to build win-win relationships. Unfortunately, the time required to do so, may be extensive, given the fact that events are typically once a month and participation by any one individual is sporadic.

Structured Networking Structured networking is a style of networking where you market your business through the development of powerful, proactive referral partners who market your business for you in return for your help in promoting their businesses. Structured networking groups, both formal and informal organizations designed to teach referral based networking and to assist in the development of teams of referral partners, have sprung up to assist in this process. Structured networking is team marketing or collaborative marketing. In structured networking, individuals interested in growing their businesses get together several times a month to learn about each other so they can promote each other within their sphere of influence.

Structured networking is a multiplicative model. Those involved work closely with a small number of like minded individuals who want to grow their businesses and are willing to work together to do so. The goal is to train a team of "referral partners" who will promote your business within their sphere of influence and to those with whom they come into contact during their daily routine. Thus, instead of networking one-on-one, structured networkers reach out to hundreds or perhaps thousands of individuals with the help of their networking team.

One of the major advantages of marketing through referral partners is that prospects are being contacted by friends, not strangers. This creates a level of acceptance that does not normally exist in the relationship between a sales person and a prospective client When you meet with someone who was referred to you, you are viewed less as a salesperson and more as a problem solver. Your credentials are assumed. The prospect is more willing to accept what you say and to follow your advice. Thus, the closing ratio is higher, price resistance is lower and the average sale is higher.

Different Skills, Different Results The skill set necessary to be an effective structured networker is very different than that required for traditional networking. Traditional networking requires you to be able to present yourself and your business effectively. Structured networking requires, in addition, that you teach others to present your business effectively. Structured networking also necessitates teamwork.

The extra effort required to be an effective structured networker, however, leads to a higher level of return. While traditional networking might account for 5% to 10% of business for most business professionals, structured networking often accounts for 30% to as much as 90% of new business. For many, it is the single most effective marketing tool they employ.

Because structured networking is a multiplicative rather than linear model and because it leverages the credibility referral partners have within their sphere of influence, it is a far more productive model than traditional networking. It does not supplant traditional networking, however. They are complementary.

http://www.NetworkingSeries.com Get 52 video clips and free tips from -Minesh Baxi and Chuck Gifford, authors of "Network Your Way To $100,000 And Beyond."

Minesh Baxi

Sure Fire Ways to Meeting New People When Networking

Meeting new people to a lot of people is intimidating. That's why a lot of people end up mingling with their friends and colleagues that they already know and comfortable with in networking events. But this is a waste of time as networking is all about meeting new people and creating business and helping other people; staying by a friend's side and socialising is not networking. Getting all dressed up, driving to the event, even paying for the event should not be wasted and should be put to best use to get to know new people and form new connections which would potentially create new business.

5 Sure fire ways to meeting new people

1. Go alone Go to the event alone so that you have no choice but to meet and mingle with new people at the event.

2. Seat at the unoccupied table By sitting at the unoccupied table you will most likely be talking to the first person who seats at the same table after you and then be joined in the conversation by the next people who will be seating at the same table.

3. Approach the person by themselves To gain greater success, approach a person standing alone. Walk up to them with a smile and introduce yourself.

4. Ask the organizer for help Upon arrival to the networking event, ask the organizer questions such as Who's here? Who should I know? Will you introduce me? So that you can strategically know who are the people you need to know at the event and be introduced to them also.

5. Serve in a committee or join a networking group Join a group you like and serve in the committee or become a board member and serve, even volunteer. This is one of the best ways of meeting new people and forming great connections with like minded people.

Now don't think it's all business, also talk to people about their hobbies or their next holiday vacations, and don't just preoccupy yourself with collecting as much business card as possible, stop and spend some time getting to know a few of them especially the right people you need to know. Meeting new people is not about stepping out of your comfort zone but expanding it. You may not be the best talker but even if you don't have much to say but you're an excellent listener, then you'll have a good networking night.

Do you want to discover more amazing Business Networking techniques, tips and strategies you need to be successful for FREE?

Get More Business, Leads And Sales when you visit: http://www.networkingsuccessecrets.com .

Larissa Martin

The 10 Biggest Networking Mistakes

Ever wish you had a time machine so you could travel back to a networking event to take back those horrible things you said? Have you ever engaged in a stimulating conversation with someone before you really know who you 're talking to, only to find out that you 've been saying the wrong things to the wrong person? Maybe you 're simply challenged by trying to eat, hold your drink, shake hands and pass out business cards all at the same time.

Well, you 're not alone. We 've all made mistakes at networking events, because - by their very nature - there are a lot of things that can go wrong .IF you 're not prepared! I have found that being prepared can help even the most socially inept, insecure or nervous person to come across like the talented professional they really are. As the author of "The Art of the Business Lunch ~ Building Relationships Between 12 and 2" (Career Press), I personally hosted more than 3,000 client lunches and attended more than 1000 networking events. I saw my sales increase by more than 2000%!

I am a professional keynote speaker and enjoy sharing "The Art of Successful Networking" with my audiences. I've found that most people have the same questions and fears, and that MOST of us are nervous or uncomfortable when put into a room full of strangers.

So, what are the biggest mistakes anyone can make at a networking event? I 'm glad you asked! Here are my Top 10 Biggest Networking Mistakes. □ If you 're like most of us, you 'll identify with at least a few of these points. Once you know what to avoid, I 'll bet you will actually look forward to the tremendous opportunities that await you at your next event.

Surely one little drink won 't hurt! □

Think again. Getting drunk or even a little sloppy in front of new acquaintances can ruin your chances of ever winning them over. Bad ideas start to sound good when you 're tipsy and you may even become inclined to share off-color jokes or reveal confidences that could sink your career. Drinking clouds your judgment, so take it easy! A great technique for cocktail mixers is to order something light and alternate with water or plain soda.

Make sure you eat something first!

You want to be able to focus on the conversation and meeting new people. You can 't do that with your mouth full of chicken or meatballs. If you 're off to a networking luncheon, remember that you can always stop and grab a bite on your way back to your office or your next sales call. And if you 're attending a cocktail mixer, grab a bite to eat as soon as you get there. I assure you it is IMPOSSIBLE to juggle a plate of food, a napkin, a cocktail, business cards (giving and receiving) AND shake hands. Remember that lunch was hours ago and any alcohol will be hitting an empty stomach! You 're likely to get drunk quickly. If possible, eat something on your way there. Worst case scenario? The food at the mixer is fabulous and you 're not hungry enough to pig out on all of it. When you arrive, head for the food, eat what you want, and then head over to the bar for your drink. You will be better able to network once you 've had a bite to eat, plus you 'll have a free hand for card exchanges and handshakes.

NEVER talk with food in your mouth!

When I was writing my book, The Art of the Business Lunch, ' absolutely everyone told me to include this advice. Apparently there are many business professionals who don 't know not to talk with their mouths full! Also, it 's good to take small bites so that if you are called upon to speak, you can quickly chew and swallow your food before speaking.

Always be kind and courteous to everyone, no matter what!

Servers are people, too. Being rude to someone, even if they 've just spilled a drink on you, only makes you look bad. Remember that any networking event is an opportunity for people to get to know you. Do you want them to come away thinking you 're nasty or over-stressed? Accidents happen. How we react to them reveals our character. This is easier to remember when things are going well. Having a great reaction when things are bad is an opportunity to impress those around you.

NEVER bad-mouth your competition.

People aren 't stupid; they will figure out that if you are saying bad things about your competition, you may say bad things about them, too, when they aren 't looking. You can build better business relationships by out-servicing and out-performing your competition.

AVOID awkward silence by being prepared for casual conversation.

Whenever I suggest being prepared for casual conversation, my audiences are surprised that they never thought to do this! Over the course of 3,000 client lunches, I learned that I had better be well informed on a LOT of different topics. Try to watch 20 minutes of a national morning news show, read a variety of magazines including industry-specific publications, and be up on the latest in pop culture. Also, be up-to-date on industry news. This should give you a wide platform of knowledge so that you can participate in nearly any conversation. And avoid any controversial subjects ; especially in a political year!

Always tip generously! Whether the networking event you 're attending has a cash bar or a hosted bar, always tip your bartender or server generously. Not only is it the right thing to do, but it 's important to take care of the people who are taking care of you. If a new associate perceives you as cheap, they may be put off.

Don 't sit with your friends.

One of the hardest things for most of us to do is to mingle with strangers. We naturally gravitate toward our personal comfort zone, which means seeking out those people we already know and hanging out with them. While a networking event offers the opportunity to see old friends and associates, the main purpose is to meet new people so you can expand your circle. If you cling to the people you already know, how can you meet anyone new? There are several things you can do to overcome your reluctance to visit with strangers, including acting as though it was your party. Playing host or hostess is a great trick; bring a plate of appetizers or desserts over to your table or offer to get drinks for everyone. This makes a strong, incredibly positive impression.

Don 't criticize ANYTHING!

We 've all been served terrible fare at networking events. Politicians joke about the endless rubber chicken □ dinners they attend while on the campaign trail. Making a big deal about a lousy buffet or fishy-smelling sushi appetizers won 't just leave a bad taste in your mouth! Those around you who may not have such a cultivated palate will be turned off, too. Everything ; from the room to the turnout to the food should be referred to as exceptional □ or outstanding. □ People prefer to be around positive people, so always try to be positive about everything.

Take your business cards or stay home! I have been handed many a phone number scribbled on a cocktail napkin. I promptly throw them away. A networking event is for business and cards are essential for so many reasons. They offer your name, your position or title, your company name, and various ways to contact you, including e-mail, direct phone line and even a cell phone number. A company website on your card eliminates any guesswork for someone who wants to know more about you or your company. Keep a stash of cards in your car so that if you run out or forget, you will have some handy. Enjoying a social setting with new friends and associates is the best way to develop relationships. Between breakfasts, lunches and cocktail mixers, the average professional has more than 400 opportunities each year to meet new people and expand their network. Being prepared for these opportunities and knowing what behavior to avoid is the first step toward guaranteeing your networking success.

Robin Jay is a professional keynote speaker, award-winning author and corporate trainer. Robin is not just the Queen of the Business Lunch, □ but is a business relationship expert who shares the nuts-and-bolts of building profitable business relationships. Her book, The Art of the Business Lunch ~ Building Relationships Between 12 and 2 □ (Career Press, 2006) has been sold in ten languages worldwide. She is a contributor to The POWER of Mentorship □ (POM) series of books, including The Millionaire Within □ and For the Woman Entrepreneur, □ and is also a contributor to the famed Chicken Soup for the Soul □ franchise of books with her entry in Chicken Soup for the Wine Lover 's Soul □ (Nov, 2007). Jay will also be a featured expert in The POWER of Mentorship: The MOVIE, □ due out December 6th, 2007. Robin is president of the Las Vegas Convention Speakers Bureau. For more information or to book Robin to speak at an event, visit her at http://www.RobinJay.com

Robin Jay

The 2006 Independent Amazon Booksellers' Convention and the Value of Professional Networking

The 2006 Independent Amazon Booksellers' Convention began last Friday (8/11/06) and just ended a few hours ago. In attendance were online booksellers representing the entire spectrum of inventory levels, product and service providers for online booksellers, and a host of personnel representing Amazon.com.

We had a "get to know one another" social gathering on Friday evening followed by presentations and working group meetings on Saturday. Sunday we were given a number of presentations by Amazon.com representatives covering many of the topics of interest to independent online booksellers. Monday (today), we were given the undivided attention of six Amazon.com vice presidents during the morning session, and we were visited by Jeff Bezos. This afternoon, we were shown some of the new products/services that Amazon.com will be releasing in the future.

I don't think I can overemphasize the value of this convention in terms of information exchanged or how much I learned. I wrote the book, "Online Bookselling: A Practical Guide with Detailed Explanations and Insightful Tips," but it was clear to me that there is even more to learn. I think it demonstrates the fact that even the author of what has been referred to by many customers as the most comprehensive book available on the topic of online bookselling can still learn more. This is exactly the type of "continuing education" I plan to incorporate into my newsletter and I appreciate the information contributions that I have been getting.

Some of the things that stood out to me were the quality and quantity of independent booksellers represented, the outstanding third party vendors of products and services oriented to assist independent online booksellers, and the level of interest and participation that Amazon.com played in the convention. That said, the highlight of the event to me personally was the opportunity to meet so many of my book customers and the supportive and appreciative feedback I got from them. It is flattering to learn that one of your first customers actually has over 2,500,000 books online and he not only tells you some of things he liked about your book, but he tells you that he learned a few things from it too. I was even asked by one of Amazon.com's Product Managers to show him my "Bookkeeping for Booksellers" software and asked to schedule a visit to present it to a gathering of Amazon.com engineers. I cannot tell you how much I appreciate the feedback and comments I got from all of these people.

Anyway, if you are serious about online bookselling I want to encourage you to put this event on next year's calendar. It doesn't matter if you have 200 books in your inventory or 10,000,000, there are people at this event that can not only teach you a thing or two, they are genuinely nice and supportive of one another. For example, I had the great privilege of meeting Dave Anderson, the owner of ScoutPal and Kevin O'Brien, the owner of SpaceWare (the provider of AMan Pro). Both are highly respected in the online bookselling community, both have great products/services, and both are very nice guys that provide fantastic support regardless of your inventory level. I spoke with both of them at length, and until later in our conversations, neither had a clue who I was even though both later acknowledged knowing about the existence of my book.

As a result of the many presentations, interactions, and discussions I was a part of over the past few days, I will have a lot to discuss in my upcoming newsletter. I even have a few wholesale/remainder book distributors to add to the already exhaustive list that is given in my book, and there were some new third-party solution providers at the convention that I will be discussing.

The newsletter will be covering all facets of the convention except those parts that Amazon.com presented and asked that we not reveal things about their upcoming product/service releases. I do not wish to jeopardize the confidence of Amazon.com or the convention organizers.

Incidentally, I would like to express my sincere thanks to Rhonda S., and Robert G., for all the work they put into organizing the entire evvent, as well as Thomas P. of Amazon for his coordination efforts.

If you want to learn more about online bookselling or my upcoming newsletter, please visit => http://www.online-bookselling.com

Michael E. Mould is the author of "Online Bookselling: A Practical Guide with Detailed Explanations and Insightful Tips," [CD-ROM ISBN 1599714876 & Paperback ISBN 1427600708] as well as the developer of "Bookkeeping for Booksellers," ISBN 1427600694.

You can ask Michael questions at: mike@online-bookselling.com

Michael Mould

The Advantages of Business Networking

Business networking is more than just a tactic that some people use to draw in more clientele. For most small business owners, proper networking skills are necessary for their continued existence and success.

Networking takes many forms. Whether a business owner is cold-calling clients on the phone, or meeting other business owners in the area for breakfast or lunch, the networking never stops. Networking leads to referral business, and referral business leads to increased customer satisfaction and loyalty.

Many owners choose to become part of organizations such as their local Chamber of Commerce. The Chamber is an excellent way for business owners to participate in business advocacy and lobbying efforts, and provides a way for business owners to band together for their own protection. Chambers of Commerce around the world hold both formal meetings and informal "meet-and-greets" during which business owners can discuss the current business climate in their given area, and formulate ways to overcome obstacles such as local governmental regulations and workforce problems.

Regardless of the type of networking activities that an owner conducts, they are still responsible for presenting themselves in a way that is both professional and forceful. Without a forceful but polite demeanor, business owners may fall prey to the most difficult of obstacles, word of mouth and the rumor mill. If a business owner doesn't conduct themselves with the utmost dignity, they may be labeled as unstable, and other business owners may elect to exclude them from future meetings and planning sessions. This leads to a rapid breakdown in communication, and a corresponding drop in sales.

An owner that is well-versed in networking skills can be nearly assured a profitable business climate and a steady stream of both new customers and repeat business. While new customers are essential to grow any business, repeat customers are equally important, as they keep the business going even during lean economic times.

Networking skills tend to be a mixture of both learned behavior and natural charisma. A business owner that can harness both aspects of the networking trade can maintain an intricate web of contacts and vendors. With that network in place, new business can always be found and the business owner can always ensure that they are being presented with the best options available to guarantee the success of their endeavors.

The author of this article is Tref Griffiths who is the CEO of the online speed-networking website http://www.networkology.com

Tref Griffiths

The Advantages of Social Networking

It's great to have friends but you have to admit that there are certain interests you or they have, which neither is not interested in. When this happens, it is time to expand our circle and that is just one of the advantages of social networking.

Social networking enables people who share the same interests to hang out together and this simply means that you are able to make new friends. If for example you are interested in basketball, no one there will get tired of talking about the players or the game which occurred last night or several years ago.

Since most social networking is done over the web, you get to meet individuals from other countries and learn about their culture. How many people do you know keep in touch with someone across the Atlantic or the Pacific? Given that you share something in common, you get to communicate with that person regularly that is very similar to hooking up with your friends after work or school.

From a business point of view, the first two advantages of social networking enable you to meet new clients and expand your business because most of these sites allow you to customize your webpage and provide links to your personal website.

Just to give you a few examples, there is Multiply, MySpace, Friendster, FaceBook and Classmates. With so many around, you won't have a hard time looking for a social network that you like. You can even post ads here so you can inform other members of an event that you are hosting.

The best part about becoming a member of a social network is that majority of these is free. This means that you don't have to pay any fees. All you have to do is sign up by filling up the form and then activating the link when this is sent to you via email. Now that you are a member, you can invite other friends to join and look at other profiles.

The advantages of social networking will allow you to make new friends, promote your business and best of all, won't cost you a thing. But there are some social networking sites that will require you to pay a fee. Before you sign up, consider if this value for your money.

Will social networking sites ever replace meeting people in social events and other gatherings? Of course not because all this medium does is give you more exposure. It allows you to put your best qualities out there especially when first impressions last.

When you join a social networking site, never post any private information about yourself unless you are ready to have people get in touch with you. You shouldn't also put anything embarrassing about yourself because some people have been denied employment because of the information posted.

If there are "privacy" settings in your social networking site, you are advised to use it so you can control who has access to your personal information.

A lot of experts say that social networking is here to stay so we have to take advantage of it. When you do join a social networking site, keep an open and see if this is exactly what you wanted. If not, cancel your account until you find the one that you like.

William Allen Yap

The Art of Networking and Business Cards

Every day we meet new people. It doesn 't matter how it happens or why it does, but it is essential to notice that we are constantly connecting with fresh faces. These new countenances could be our future employer, a potential best friend, or simply another person to pass on our services to. With hundreds of meetings each month, it is no surprise that the public is now taking advantage of these meet and greets.

Business networking is a great way to make connections with others. Although we meet new people on a daily basis, we don 't always keep the relationship going. We all want to be known in our specialized field. Therefore, having an array of business cards would create more opportunities and a plethora of open doors.

If you are running a small or large business, then it is necessary to have a great business card. One must always remember that this is an affordable way to advertise your services. It doesn 't have to be extravagant. However, it does need to include vital information such as a phone number, e-mail address and website address if you have one. Many people also prefer to spice it up with a bit of color. After all, color business cards will most certainly stand out in a pile of black and white cards.

It is very important to remember that business cards are piece of paper that is marketing your services. It should reflect your company 's image and of course portray the type of feeling you want. For instance, if you are an artist, it would be wise to create a professional yet artsy business card. Perhaps a colored business card with a logo of your art work would show others that you are ready to work for them.

By handing them out to anyone you meet, you are setting up a new contact. Even if you do not see them again, they will still have your business card. Therefore, you 'll never know when they will need your expertise. They may even contact you when a job opening is available or when another client of theirs is in desperate need of great service in your field.

It is extremely simple to create them yourself. Most drug stores carry business card paper which is usually only a few dollars. Many stores even have patterns and color business cards in a variety of hues. This will allow you to be creative and make your piece of paper stand out! If you are computer literate, it is easy to design everything on the computer and then print it out with the paper you bought. There are special printing options for business cards, so it is crucial to change the preferences beforehand. On the other hand, if you are too busy or computer illiterate, perhaps you should hire a professional to create your business cards. There are many businesses including Kinko 's, who will design a wonderful color business card for an affordable price.

Although business cards sound like a hassle for some, they are actually one of the most affordable marketing tools for your company. Most businesses get ahead easily if they are constantly offering people their business cards. It is not only a great way to make connections, but it also lets you know that you have done everything in your power to get clients.

http://www.latenightprinters.com

Natalie Aranda writes on small business and marketing . Business networking is a great way to make connections with others. Although we meet new people on a daily basis, we don 't always keep the relationship going. We all want to be known in our specialized field. Therefore, having an array of business cards would create more opportunities and a plethora of open doors. It is extremely simple to create them yourself. Most drug stores carry business card paper which is usually only a few dollars. Many stores even have patterns and color business cards in a variety of hues. This will allow you to be creative and make your piece of paper stand out!

Natalie Aranda

The Dawn of Social Networking and Blogging Sites

No doubt has an individual's personal life dramatically changed from writing down one's thoughts and feelings on a notebook known as a diary to posting pictures, videos and blogs of one's life in a webpage. This is yet another full proof of how technology and the internet have made its impact in our daily lives a nd how globalization spread outs in different fields.

The function of both technology and the internet in our present society continuously expands and attracts people from the many walks of life. And with the introduction of social networking and blogging sites, more and more people are being drawn to the magic of the internet. This doesn't only holds true towards kids and teenagers but for adults as well.

Social networking and blogging sites initially had the youth as its captured market. And since this has now developed into profit generating means, those beyond their 20's have engaged in the use of these internet-based recreations.

But what pros and cons has this new era of internet-based innovation brought about to the society? For globalization and reaching out to people, this has by far made a really great impact on how we go about socialization. Individuals can now keep in touch with people they haven't seen or heard from for a very long time. They can also get connected with complete strangers form different countries who wish to acquire as many friends as they wish or relatives who are in a different country. This is also a means to speak one's mind and be visible. At the same time it is used as venue to brainstorm questions and answers to the millions of information and topics around the globe. A large number of people have taken advantage of this by simply making money out of just sharing thoughts and opinions. As for this part, it doesn't sound bad at all.

On the other side of the fence, reality check, once anyone posts anything on the internet through these sites, one has agreed to publicize certain aspects of his life that used to be known just among family, closest friends or professional contacts. It is true that these sites have encourage connectedness and globalization in a different aspect, but take note of the fact that this kind is more on a very personal level. A very personal level, that at times not even an individual's parents are aware of these unless they have read or since it in one of those social networking sites. And not to forget the attacks on sensitive information such as password and credit card information. There are also concerns regarding harassment over these sites. In addition, this has also brought about lower productivity and more conflicts due to excessive use of use sites even during working hours.

Both social networking and blogging has its benefits and drawbacks. A remind for anyone and everyone to take precautions while enjoying this perks of the internet. So if you're the type of individual who values privacy too much, be extra careful in venturing into this. It has made both money and friends for a lot but it has also caused a lot of trouble for some. This significant era of internet-based technology and feature have more in store for the world in the future and millions are continuously patronizing it. It would always be better to learn and understand it before jumping into it or even if you're already a part of it.

Taina Uy is a visual and literal artist, who dabbles back and forth between spinning stories and drawing things. She's a big fan of digital arts, and is into web design and digital painting. Should you want to get started on creating your own website as a part of your eBusiness plan, start out with these SiteGrinder video tutorials .

Visit her SiteGrinder website for more information.

Taina Uy

The Importance of Maintaining a Professional Image on Social Networking Sites

With the recent growth of social networking sites such as My Space and Facebook, online self expression has become the latest trend. Many individuals dedicate countless hours, days, and even months trying to create social networking pages that give outsiders a bird 's eye view of their thoughts and personal beliefs. While on one hand, social networking sites can be used to promote a positive cause or professional business, too much of a good thing can be detrimental to one 's career and professional image.

Gone are the days when social networking meant exactly what it stands for. These days, social networking sites can be used to promote professional businesses, organizations, and other causes. Members of these sites have also begun creating pages that contain pornographic pictures and other offensive imaging. If you are 18-20 years old and a member of the, Girls Gone Wild □ group, it may be fun for now, but what about your future? For example, a recent news story describes how a police officer was fired because of offensive imaging on his MySpace page, which consisted of pictures of women being tortured in a satanistic manner. Although, these social networking sites take preventative measures, it is still up to the individual to take responsibility for themselves and the images and content that they post on their webpages. In this particular case, this is especially true because of the type of value system and beliefs, police officers in the local community strive to represent. A police 's professional image plays a huge role in the public 's opinion of that individual and the police department.

The same holds true for other professional companies and organizations. In order to prevent being embarrassed by prospective employees, employers have begun doing background checks on these individuals. Many employers have refused to hire individuals that post offensive pictures and other material on their personal webpages. While some critics disagree, the reasoning is simple: employees are apart of the organization, therefore, employees represent the organization. This not only applies during work hours but after work as well. When an employee working for a major company embarrasses themselves, by disgracing themselves in public, it is also embarrassing for the company or any other organizations that individual is associated with.

How can this be avoided? As an individual, it is always important to remember the importance of a good reputation. It is said, that it takes years to build a good reputation and only moments to ruin it. Credibility and reliability are key aspects of building a good reputation. Understanding the importance of weighing the consequences of our decisions and considering our long term goals is especially important when trying to project a professional image. The solution is simple, when creating personal webpages, think of the consequences that may result from posting images that may be offensive to others. No one wants to lose the opportunity of a life time because of pictures from their spring break in college. Before you post these images consider your future and how others will view you as an individual and a professional.

Kristy K. Taylor

The Importance of Networking

Everyone knows how important personal networking is right? If you do not know, you most certainly should!

The more people you know and maintain a good relationship with people the more likely they are to call you up and let you know about opening opportunities. Friends share with friends, that is a basic thing we are all taught from the moment we end up at our first day of school. The most important thing friends may share with friends is information.

Yeah, I know how crazy that sounds!

Information is so important that the entire internet was based on the concept that people would be able to quickly share important and not-so-important information with one another. Of course, radio, the telephone, and television are also examples of information-sharing technologies. People like to share what is going on with one another. That is just a fact. Which is proven time and time again, just look at the popularity and success of these recent "reality" shows on television.

The same concept has been used over and over: the sharing of information equals profit. So, the more people you know the more you can profit. Opportunities come and go, but the more people you maintain a decent relationship with the more people that are going to be willing to share the opportunities that they know about with you!

This is another reason why it is important, and maybe even more important, to make friends while managing to work hard at your job. It may sound a little like exploiting people for their good nature, but this is simply understanding how the world really works. It is just revealing a few of the fishing lines really holding up the stars in the background.

Jimmy Callahan

The Importance of Networking

"In life, it is not what you know or who you know that counts - it is both!" - Anthony J. D'Angelo

When you're looking for a job, having connections makes the process much easier. Given two candidates with the same qualifications, the hiring manager is more likely to choose the one that comes with a recommendation from a colleague. A sparkling testimonial is a powerful thing.

This phenomenon also holds true in the business world. Making connections can open lots of doors that may have otherwise been slammed in your face. Let's take a look at some of the things networking can do for you.

Finding New Customers

One of the most obvious advantages of business networking is that it can help us find new customers. Building a rapport with others who may need what you have to offer can help build your customer base. If you needed a product or service, wouldn't you prefer to go to someone you know and trust if that were an option?

Even those who have no need for what we have to offer can bring us business. They have their own network of contacts, and there's a good probability that they know someone who could use your goods or services. Even if they do not, they might meet someone some day who does, and when that time comes, they will know who to recommend.

Forming Joint Ventures

Those who serve your target market in a different capacity than you can help you find new customers. But you may also be able to help one another in a different way: by combining your efforts into a joint venture.

A good joint venture can bring far better results than two individual campaigns. You can share the costs and work with the other party, cutting your investments of both time and money in half. And the rewards can be great. Both parties can reach portions of their target market that they may not have reached otherwise, and that could easily translate to more sales.

Learning from One Another

There's more to networking than finding ways to directly make money. Getting to know fellow entrepreneurs can be a learning experience. You might stumble upon just the piece of advice you've been looking for, or you may even find a mentor.

But remember, it's a two-way street. If you want to benefit from the knowledge of those who are more experienced than you, you need to do your part to help others who can benefit from your knowledge. You reap what you sow.

How Does Networking Work?

"When we seek for connection, we restore the world to wholeness. Our seemingly separate lives become meaningful as we discover how truly necessary we are to each other." - Margaret Wheatley

It's not hard to understand why networking is a good thing. But to the uninitiated, the very idea of it can be confusing and intimidating. You might find yourself asking questions like:

• Where do I go to meet fellow businesspeople? • What do I say when I meet them? • How can I make sure they remember me? • What if I make a bad impression?

Even the most socially adept have been known to get butterflies in their stomachs when it comes to business networking. It's natural. But don't let it stop you from making connections that could help you achieve more.

Meeting fellow businesspeople is easy enough. You can find them at functions hosted by your local Chamber of Commerce or small business organization, and at trade shows. Online, there are lots of forums and networking groups consisting of businessmen and women that you can become a part of.

Knowing what to say when you meet someone you would like to network with may be a little more difficult. Small talk is okay, but it won't get you very far. You need to hit them with something that makes you stand out from the crowd. This is where an elevator speech comes in handy.

Your elevator speech is a short yet powerful description of what you do. The question is bound to come up, and if you merely answer with your profession, you've lost an important opportunity. But if you have crafted an attention-grabbing elevator speech, you can seize the opportunity to highlight the benefits of your business.

As the name suggests, your elevator speech should be short enough that you could make it during an elevator ride. But you can use it in any networking situation. It shouldn't be a sales pitch, but it should be engaging and make the listener eager to learn more about who you are and what you do.

A good elevator speech will help you make a good first impression. If either party is pressed for time, offering a business card will keep you fresh on the listener's mind and ensure that he knows how to contact you later. If not, your elevator speech can pave the way for a more detailed discussion.

For some, networking comes naturally. For others, it takes a little more thought and preparation. But practice makes perfect, and the more you practice, the more your network will grow.

Networking Is About Give and Take

"All men are caught in an inescapable network of mutuality." - Martin Luther King, Jr.

When networking, it is crucial to present yourself well. But it's equally important to remember that it's not all about you.

Listen to what others have to say. You might find that they offer something that you need. You might realize that you have something unique to offer them. You might know someone to whom you could refer them. Or you might see an opportunity for the two of you to help each other.

That's the beauty of networking. It's not like advertising, in which you lay out the benefits of your product or service and the audience listens passively. It's interactive. And when a connection is made, everyone involved wins.

Jeremy Gislason is the owner of SureFireWealth Inc and the publisher of the self improvement series at http://www.mindmaptoriches.com . His book "Mindmap to riches" will boost your self-confidence and get you thinking with a positive attitude daily.

Jeremy A Gislason

The Importance of Social Networking in Online Business

You have friends. Your friends have other friends. The other friends of your friends have also other friends and so on and so forth. This pattern of acquaintances and friendship can be called a network -- more specifically a social network.

But the people you call acquaintances or friends are not with you because they just happen to be with you. They have become part of your lives since you have things in common or you have the same interests.

This concept of it not only applies in the real world but also in the virtual world called the Internet. There are a lot of communities all over the information superhighway which were built because of a certain interest which are shared by each and every member.

In the old days, social networking may have just been a way to be able to meet people who have the same interests as you do. But today, it has become a very useful tool in online businesses.

Defining Social Networking

Ever since man has developed communication, this has already existed. Even today, all of us are bound by its mechanics and a very good example of this is your friends. Your group of friends alone can already be called a social network -- you have the same interests. And when you meet new people, make acquaintances and make new friends, this can be considered as social networking.

For those people who are aware of this idea can see this as an opportunity that can be taken advantage of. An example of this would be the world of business and trade. Companies and firms who share the same interests would forge ties with each other to strengthen and fortify their businesses.

Simply put, this is making connections with a person or even a group of people who share the same interests as you do.

Social Networking and Online Businesses

If it works "offline" then it would also work online. The citizens of the Internet, specifically the entrepreneurs of online business, have seen the power of social networking. Because of this, they have developed methods on how to utilize this to their advantage.

A method they have developed is called business bookmarking which is a variation of the ever so popular social bookmarking. It utilizes the power of networking online but this time in the context of businesses. It has become a very effective method for both small and big businesses who want to reach to people all over the world. With the help of the network of business bookmarking, businesses were given the opportunity to reach more people and have a bigger audience.

Just like networking in the real world, the basic rule still applies -- it is all about having the same interests. In the Internet, online businesses who have the same interest would contact each other. If all goes well, they would forge a partnership, an alliance if you may call it, to boost their status.

Vanessa A. Doctor from Jump2Top - SEO Company

http://conbuzz.com - Conbuzz

Vanessa A. Doctor

The LinkedIn Badge As a Social Networking Promotion Tool on Your Blog

Using The LinkedIn Badge To Promote Your Online Profile

You Have Finally Found Your LinkedIn Badge - That Was Hard. Where to use it, now? Well, due to the 'seriousness' of this Professional Networking portal, you are presented a very few designs available for badges.

LinkedIn offers you only ten designs, plus one more special for the TypePad users that beams you up right into the TypePad's TypeLists widget management system. You will stay put and have nothing to tweak or configure, I should say. It's straight and simple, quite spartan design.

The badge you're getting has a sole purpose: to link back to your own LinkedIn Public Profile page. Actually, it is only an image (a proprietary one) that may be added with no fuss to any online portals or social networks, blogging platform or your own sites.

Having no JavaScript (it's a html - href with an img src - tag) you'll find yourself easy to insert it into your TypePad, MySpace, or Blogger template. I'll exemplify from my direct experience with my WordPress blog. It is just the best example. Here's how I did it...

Inserting LinkedIn Badge into your WordPress Sidebar

Login as admin into your WordPress dashboard

Select Setting on the upper right side of the screen

Go on Design

Then on Widgets

And Finally the Text category with the Add Arbitrary text or HTML link

That opens the widget editor to the right   Give it a nice title like 'Look at me' or whatever you may dream of

Copy/paste the html code previously taken from LinkedIn's Badge

Go Change to the bottom-left   Then Save Changes

And Visit Site to check it

That's about all. You will have now a very nice badge inside one of the widget areas on your blog's sidebar. Nice! Go promote it! It will bring you back, in time many kinks and, of course, free traffic. Enjoy!

Steve Lorenzo The VaultBoss @ The KnowHow Vault Blog

Curious about me:

Follow me on Twitter http://twitter.com/SteveLorenzo

For more news, tricks and tips on Internet Marketing related subjects, check my blog regularly: http://www.knowhowvault.com/wordpress/

Steven Lorenzo

The Nature Of Sales Networking

Networking effectiveness starts with a positive personal attitude and an understanding that successful networking is built on a spirit of giving and sharing and not of bargaining and keeping score .

Armed with this knowledge, we can now look at how the process of good sales networking actually works in practice.

The first thing to realise about networking is that everyone you meet is a useful prospective network contact. This seemingly simple fact is often overlooked, as people engage in their own private screening process before they will talk to anyone.

There is obviously a line to be drawn between talking to anyone and everyone in the street and talking to almost no one. However, if you want to network more and to do so successfully, there are many situations that qualify as the right opportunity □.

Taking An Interest in Anybody & Everybody

It is often the case that we don 't really know very much about even close people around us (let alone distant contacts). Even if we do know a little, we are less likely to know how far or deep their skill, knowledge or resources extend. If this is true of your knowledge of others, how much do they really know about you?

Herein lays the basic secret of networking success:

-You have to become interested in anybody and everybody

-You have to share more about yourself than you may have done in the past

It is out this mutual exchange of knowledge that network contacts will connect and start to offer support, help, advice, favours, referrals and other benefits on a regular basis.

Core Processes

Developing a conscious understanding of this giving and sharing strategy can take some time and some practice.

In her book "How to master networking ', Robyn Henderson calls this process earning the right to ask a favour of another person, or giving without hooks. Both of these statements imply two processes that operate pretty much at the same time (and neither of them necessarily out first reaction).

The two processes in earning the right to ask a favour are :

-Giving away information (to be helpful)

-Being open for any help you may need

Let 's look at these two processes in turn.

Giving Away Information

Whether it is accidental or planned, formal or informal, random or structured, in discussion with other people the effective networker offers his or her knowledge, skills, ideas, resources, guidance or data freely ; without any "hooks ' or expectations that repayment is due in any form. In fact, the only immediate benefit may be the pleasure to be derived from assisting someone with information that was of value to them.

Whilst the giver expects nothing in return, the receiver has a very positive experience and memory of you upon which they can act (if they so choose) in the future. If they do, either directly or indirectly, at some indeterminate time, you may receive some reciprocal benefit.

Along with openly offering any possible help and support, the effect networker does not operate as a one-way helper or super person/white knight/angel coming to the rescue of everyone else, but never personally in need of assistance. He or she also talks realistically about personal goals, tasks, challenges, problems and general issues, and acknowledges feeling vulnerable in not being able to do everything single-handedly. Being open means being receptive to help when it is offered and, on occasions, asking networking contacts if they can suggest ideas, strategies or approaches that could assist you.

Two-Way Process

These two processes operate at the same time and together to create a cycle through which "favours ' are continually offered to all who participate. These favours are both offered and taken in order to keep the network strong and capable of growing to include more and more people.

This process is called "reciprocity '. It simply means that effective networking is a coin with two sides rather than just one. You can 't have one without the other.

Successful networking is therefore about:

-Giving and receiving

-Contributing and accepting support

-Offering and requesting

-Promoting other 's needs and promoting your own needs

-Trust and persistence

Jonathan Farrington is the Managing Partner of The jfa Group . To find out more about the author or to subscribe to his newsletter for dedicated sales professionals, visit: http://www.jonathanfarrington.com

Jonathan Farrington

The Networking Advantage

Creating, building and maintaining a personal and professional network can be a real advantage. Often these are called social, business, or professional networks to distinguish them from the information systems type.

The value of contacts with essential information can make your job, and life, easier. In critical times this network can not only be advantageous but essential.

NETWORKING

Simply stated networking is a linkage of individuals or organizations to one another. We all have informal networks which we may not realize are purposeful connections which can give us a personal, professional, or competitive advantage.

Usually networks are based on some type of affiliation. A typical network is one's network of friends. These days social networks are likely to be established in cyberspace. Note the wild success of "MySpace" and "Facebook" which permit individuals with common interests to interact in large networks. These are frequently loose affiliations with people listing themselves as "friends" who have never met and often never interacted in any meaningful fashion.

The more purposeful networking examples include professional or fraternal organizations such as: American Management Association, industry or regionally specific groups or organization chapters. The local Chamber of Commerce provides an excellent example of a networking forum where members can exchange business cards and information or make customer referrals. Also Alumni organizations, neighborhood associations and the like are common interfaces. Church groups are another effective place for contacts and networking. All of these linkages can provide resources for the participant in their business and/or personal lives.

ESTABLISH NETWORKS AT WORK

A few years back the County of Los Angeles tried an experiment. The intent was to make the government services more efficient and cost-effective. A network of managers from various agencies and departments was formed to interact and exchange information and to promote the adoption of "best practices" throughout the forty-three departments. A further element was the designation of an advisory committee recruited from private sector executives, productivity experts, and educators from local colleges to expand the network into a public/private partnership. The County managers retained their original responsibilities and roles while the Productivity Network was superimposed on the official organizations. This dual responsibility made more work for the participants but gave them new avenues of access to management in other organizations and to the business and educational communities. It was more than a committee or task force but rather a barrier-breaking, empowering social and professional system.

The results were spectacular. The effects had County government managers "thinking outside the box" and coming up with new, novel, and synergistic solutions to long-standing problems. Government budgeting and funding mechanisms do much to stifle innovation. There's no R&D in government. So, in order to inspire entrepreneurial approaches, the network developed a "Productivity Investment Fund" where members could apply for funding of projects with potential for ROI. The applications were reviewed by a Board which had the power to fund projects outside of the normal budgetary system. A competitive environment was encouraged. A portion of the savings from the successful projects was required above the initial investment payback. This "venture capital" style of approaching innovation was new to the County employees who were accustomed to more passive and familiar approaches like budget allocations and "suggestion awards." And, lots of ideas were generated while the fund grew as a result of the surplus contributions in excess of the payback of the original "investment."

Although approaches like this one are more common in the private sector they are still not employed often enough. "Gainsharing" programs where employees themselves share in the savings or income generated from implementing innovations provide additional incentive for creativity. And, when combined with networking, these programs and approaches have an even greater chance of success.

The networking advantage results from a combination of contacts, resources and ideas shared outside the formal organization structure and channels. Whether the network is formed by design, allowed to operate independently or nurtured within the organization the results are almost invariably positive and synergistic.

THE INFORMAL NETWORK

As indicated, informal networks are the most common. These pervasive affiliations in the employment arena are frequently more powerful than the official organizations. The networks based on personal contacts can serve to expedite the tasks and processes of the organization without reverting to the "chain of command." Arrangements like these create a more fluid and adaptive organization. After all, most human interaction is based on relationships regardless of formal structure.

Many a naÃ¯ve manager has run afoul of the informal organization through an unawareness or lack of appreciation of these networks.

THE PROFESSIONAL NETWORK

Members of a trade or profession frequently join forces to enjoy the benefits of referral business and access to required resources or services. For example, in Miami there is an extended group engaged in the construction, trades, renovation, and home improvement businesses who share purchasing resources, general and sub-contract with one another, and refer customers to each other. This model is constantly used with businesses throughout the business world. Preferred suppliers, rebates for referrals, joint ventures, structured "partnerships," etc., are all variations on this theme. And there are many more. Of course they are all based on a networking model which benefits each and every participant and typically the customer as well. Because the reputation of each participant is dependent on the quality of the services and workmanship of the others there is a sort of "self policing" in operation.

SOME NETWORKING TIPS

The ubiquitous nature of networking and the power of this approach combine to make this an important asset in the managerial arsenal. Here are some tips to making your networking efforts more successful:

First, realize that networking is everywhere in the business and personal areas of life.

Second, recognize the potential for payoff in the networking approach, especially in gaining awareness, recognition and in marketing your products and services.

Third, foster networking by keeping in contact with your friends, colleagues, and Business associates.

Fourth, join and participate in groups that will provide you with essential or meaningful contacts and resources.

Fifth, regularly exchange business cards, telephone numbers and email addresses.

Sixth, consider the initiation of contrived, purposeful networks (like the example from L.A. County).

Seventh, check out Internet business networking sights such as fastpitchnetworking.com.

Eighth, establish a referral network to share information and customers among naturally related businesses, and actively promote these linkages.

Ninth, initiate prompt corrective action when network members fail in their responsibilities and obligations, or if necessary sever counter-productive relationships. Such problems can adversely impact all members of the network.

Tenth, enjoy and reap the benefits of your active participation in networking activities.

Ben A. Carlsen, Ed.D, MBA, is an experienced CEO and manager. Dr. Carlsen has over 30 years experience in management, consulting, and teaching. Currently the Head of the Business Department at Everest Institute, Hialeah, FL., he was Chairman of the Los Angeles County Productivity Managers Network and President of the Association for Systems Management (So. Calif. Chapter). Additional information can be obtained at http://drben.info

Ben Carlsen

The Networking Boomerang - 6 Ways to Maximize Your People Power

Networking--is realizing the power of cooperation instead of competition and linking people and information together for the mutual benefit of everyone involved.

Do you know what's given "networking" a bad reputation? Those that are out there selling in the name of networking--cold hard selling. Those that have mastered the correct concept of networking, however, do so in a quiet, yet powerful manner, using the power of both grace and respect.

Understand and develop that personal power within you, and your network becomes unlimited! Here are 6 important steps to help you become a respected influential networker:

1. The power of giving has a "boomerang effect" and is a sure guarantee of networking. In other words, what you give will always come back in some form because that is the law of giving. However, someone must always take the first action of giving and "throw the boomerang" for it to return.

Due to the fact that human nature naturally responds to giving by giving back, the simple act of this can be a powerful way to activate your network. Never pass up a chance to give support to others, raise the level of the discussion, provide value, or offer solutions; then watch for the boomerang and be ready to catch it when it returns.

2. Expand your thinking beyond yourself. Make the change from thinking that you can work your business successfully on your own, and shift toward the mentality that you can accomplish greater things when you work effectively with others.

Don't limit your outreach and effectiveness as a networker. You yourself are a valued source of resources and contacts. You have a unique store of connections and life experiences that provide an unlimited wealth of knowledge and opportunities. Share those with others and draw from the experience of others as well. Everyone brings unique value to the table.

3. Praising yourself and others brings people to a higher level of energy and awareness. We all thrive on positive reinforcement. Focusing on the strengths of others develops winners and leaders.

Send notes frequently that say "thanks for the support....thanks for your friendship....thanks for the referral...for the words of encouragement...for the opportunity to learn about your business...for the opportunity to do business with you...for taking the time to...." Specifically tell people how they influence your life in a positive way. There is much power in praise!

4. We all have a vast network; but some of those connections may have become weak and neglected. Take some time to reconnect and polish up those communication connections. Networking can be as simple as a friendship. Don't complicate it. It's all about being there for each other.

I like the phrase that says "people are much more likely to be people loyal than they are to be brand loyal." Don't underestimate the power of your contacts! Your network will be able to grow more naturally as you strengthen your relationships and keep them nurtured.

5. Listening....the heart of communication; don't view this important tool to communication as simply a matter of not talking. Listening is all about being mentally engaged in what the other person is saying, giving your full attention to someone else to create a connection that goes beyond the words being spoken. Listening is where people develop rapport and trust.

Even when there is nothing in it for you, listening and responding accordingly to people will help strengthen those relationships and will reap rewards that will come in the future. Be aware of non-business needs you can fill as well. There are always opportunities to recommend a dentist, a hair stylist, an auto mechanic, a travel agent, etc.

6. Commitment is the breaker between a mediocre networker and a master networker. Networking is absolutely what has to be done to produce good results in any network marketing business.

It is the most cost-effective network marketing tool for reaching an endless stream of influential contacts and growing your business. Good ideas will not produce results-daily actions and habits will. Make a commitment to yourself, your relationships, and these powerful networking principles and you will be moving toward a life of richness, blessed by both a vast network of support and friendships, as well as a growing successful business.

Networking is like a treasure hunt-searching for the jewels that are out there, just not knowing where. So you meet one person, talk to another person, call up that person, and then you find a jewel! Let networking be fun! Treat it with respect and it will boomerang back to you producing incredible results!

Katie Liljeberg is an online network marketer who discovered how to build a massive organization without using the old-fashioned traditional network marketing techniques. To learn the secrets, visit: http://www.KatieLive.com

Katie Liljeberg

The Networking Scorecard

In recent years the opportunity to extend your influence, develop connections and build relationships beyond your immediate circle of associates, colleagues and friends has been made a lot easier thanks to the development of multiple online networks and the proliferation of clubs, societies and groups on your doorstep. Indeed, just in the last month, three new "networks" have launched in my town creating three new opportunities for me to eat breakfast, lunch and dinner with local business owners, discussing opportunities, sharing knowledge and making referrals. Alternatively, I could look at them as three new opportunities to distract me from the short-term objective of getting money into my business.

So, where to start? The answer, as is often the case when a strategic problem arises, is at the end. You need to decide what you want to achieve out of your networking? Is it a 50% improvement to the bottom-line or is it to gain access to a specific group or individual? Is it to build the profile of your business in advance of an AIM listing or is it to build your knowledge and skills with a group of like-minded people? Whatever your reasons, you need to write them down. Once your goal is clear, you will find that your decisions and activities will also become more focused. Now it's just a case of chipping away at your goal, one new connection at a time.

Whenever I am in conversation with someone who is considering becoming better networked I always advise them that networking will deliver at best a medium term return on their investment. True there are innumerable intangible benefits on the way such as new friendships, exciting new insights and a lot of fun, but for those who are results oriented these can be inconsequential and frustrating distractions. The key is to stay focused but leave the door open for serendipity. For example, one client of mine was so focused on gaining access to the key influencers inside his target retail client that he turned down the opportunity to attend a charity golf event as it did not involve anyone from the industry and was mostly attended by retired "city" guys. The local paper covered the event the following week, and there, holding up the winners cup was the Finance Director from his target client - apparently a late replacement for his father (you guessed it, a retired "city" guy). It took my client another eight long months before he finally developed a relationship that got him into his target organization. Sometimes you walk by the right ones because you're trying too hard to see them. Remember, you can count the seeds in an apple but you can't count the apples in the seed.

Once you've set your networking goal, here's a 5 Step plan to achieve it.

1) Plan for each event - this needn't take hours, just get the attendee list, highlight the individuals you would like to talk to, grab your business cards and get going. Even this amount of planning will put you ahead of 95% of the other people there!

2) Make a memorable first impression - if you are genetically outside of average, this can be ticked off straight away (you wouldn't forget someone who is 6' 10" would you?), otherwise, what can you do to make a memorable impression? Maybe it's an item of clothing or an accessory, maybe you can practice some jokes and make people laugh, maybe you can be a great introducer or perhaps you just have a smile and a persona that lights up the room? Whatever, just ensure that you do not fade into the "wall of suits". After all, your aim when networking is for people to remember you long enough that they can refer you confidently, and if their mental image of you is a blur, you are not doing yourself any favours. Seek advice from friends and relatives until you discover something that you are comfortable with AND helps you to stand out.

3) Employ the Caring principle - remember, people don't care how much you know until they know how much you care! In the networking context that means listening to them, intently. Build rapid rapport through active and literal listening, matching body language and even speech moderation. Do whatever it takes to help the other person relax in your company and you will have the foundation of a great relationship.

4) Have some Networking Enlisting Words - and use them to help people remember what you do. Scientists have estimated that we are exposed to more than 2 million messages a day - so how can you make your message stick? The answer is, with difficulty. Remember that you are trying to develop advocates not recruit customers so be excruciatingly specific about who you help, what you do and with what results. Don't worry about all the things you don't cover with these words, people will make assumptions or ask questions if they understand at least one thing that you do. So, if you are an expert in stress relief, don't say "I can help anyone suffering with stress" because that does not help me. Instead, focus on one key ailment (maybe long-term shoulder pain) and tell me what amazing results you have achieved with a recent client. I will make the mental leap about your overall competence and maybe even ask if you also cover back pain, but more importantly, I might know or be a potential client for your shoulder services! At the next meeting, focus on another area.

5) Follow Up - or everything you have done before is wasted!

So, we've got a goal, we've even got a 5 Step implementation plan, do we need anything else? Yes we do, we need to measure our progress and success, otherwise networking will become another bucket for lost time in our business. Measurement transforms networking from an activity that we feel we ought to be doing into a powerful strategic tool. The Networking Scorecard below will get you started, email me if you'd like a formatted pdf version.

Choose a period to monitor and capture your Target and Actual totals in the spaces provided.

NETWORKING SCORECARD

Period .... - ....

Targets Actuals

BUSINESS (Bottom Line Value)

REFERRALS (Given / Received)

FOLLOW-UPS

1-2-1 MEETINGS

CONVERSATIONS

Simon D Phillips

The Networking Trifecta

The definition of trifecta means to bet on the three finishers of the race in the corrector order. It's a system that determines a certain sequence that happens in order to win.

In networking, there are three major functions that if done properly will help you win the race of getting more business.

Show Up - Most people assume that if they simply join an organization, get listed in a directory, post a profile in a social community online or attend every once and a while, that they will instantly get business pouring in. Unfortunately, that doesn't always work especially if their competition is actively involved. When it comes to networking, it's an interactive sport. Your participation is critical if you ever expect to get a return on your investment.

Follow Up - Even if you meet 50-100 people each week and you attend every event possible and you're on a ton of social networks, if you never follow up, you'll never move past the initial introduction. Don't assume someone will "sell themselves" on your products or service and call immediately to buy something. If you want something to happen, you must take the initiative to reconnect and offer continuous follow up. That means, to follow up over and over, not just one time.

Build Relationships - The secret to getting more business is simple. Get people to fall in love with you, to believe in you, and to know that you will take care of their business. The more you share of yourself and offer value to someone else, the more likely they are to remember you when it's time for them to need what you offer. When you make them feel important and value their relationship, they will become one of your "Marketing Messengers" delivering your business to people they know in their network and send you referrals.

All three of these are the keys that will help you create the Networking Trifecta and generate more business than you ever imagined.

Darlene Willman, aka The Sassy Networker, is a keynote speaker , author and coach, specializing in small business networking and referrals. She provides resources, connections and support to entrepreneurs, small business owners and other professionals that have a strong desire to promote their companies through relationship marketing. She will show you how to build an incredible network of people who refer business to each other plus so much more. You can start receiving her eZine, The Networking Focus (a $67 value) by visiting http://www.SassyNetworker.com

Contact our office today at (636) 387-3000 to book Darlene Willman as your next keynote speaker.

Darlene Willman

The Number One Networking Tip

Professionals, entrepreneurs and students study and practice networking as an art of science. It can be complex yet practical way of developing professionally and socially. They are encouraged to read articles and books as well as join clubs and organizations for active participation. There are several unwritten rules and protocols that are associated with networking. There are rules that affect the verbal and non-verbal communication queues when interacting with others. It is always recommended to have a good 30 second speech for a good first impression. It is also important to have a firm handshake as a sign of respect and protocol. It is also critical to have business cards and display card etiquette when passing them around. Among all of these tips and advice what is the most valuable networking tip?

Listed below is the best tip any Power Network can use for business and social success:

Network with Passion.

Passion defined in the dictionary clearly states, "a strong enthusiasm for something or a strong emotion or feeling." Successful people are extremely passionate about what they do. They can find ways to connect their passion with their personality, abilities and goals.

It is a networking principle that separates the amateurs from the skilled. It is a golden rule which can instantly define an individual and brands them in a positive light. It is a key characteristic to successfully reaching a goal or objective. Networking with passion is very important because it motivates the individual and provides emotional, mental and physical energy.

The tremendous benefits of being a Passionate Networker include:

#1 Being less likely to suffer from burn out. #2 Remaining focused on goals and objectives. #3 Attracting the right people and connections with positive attitudes. #4 Understanding the importance of networking. #5 Maintaining long term and meaningful relationships.

Chi Chi Okezie is owner/producer of SIMPLEnetworking, LLC in Metro-Atlanta, GA. Newly published author of "SIMPLEnetworking: Creating Opportunities ... The new form of success!" View excerpts of the book and polish your professional approach: http://www.snseminars.com

Chi Chi Okezie

The Power of Social Networking and Its Effect on Your Business

On a daily basis, millions of web browsers flock to social networking sites such as Facebook, Twitter, MySpace, Linked In, Better Networker, YouTube, and many, many others across the Internet. Just recently, Facebook reached 200 million users and that number is climbing by the hour. The average person spends 19-25 minutes per day social networking.

Due to their popularity, social networking sites provide a fantastic platform for meeting new people and expanding your skill set by learning from others. And, they can be downright addicting, too!

Many home-based business owners are using these sites as a way to market their business. But to do this effectively, there are some things you want to be aware of. It's important to treat these sites like any live networking event. When you're at a mixer or social event, you don't try to sell your business or product everyone you meet. You mingle and get to know people. Facebook, Twitter, and the others are the exact same thing and can be a tremendous asset to your home-based business if utilized correctly.

You always want be transparent on these sites. You're providing a sneak peek into your life, so don't be afraid to share your story, hobbies, interests, favorite books and movies, and goals. Always provide a way for people to check out your business, but don't blatantly throw it in their face. Once someone gets to know you, they'll naturally be interested in what you do.

In addition, as I mentioned before, don't try to blatantly sell your product or business opportunity. This is a tremendous turn-off and people will quickly ignore you. Instead, interact with people you share common ground with on other levels, such as opinions on a movie or favorite sports team. Any social gathering you attend is not filled with people peddling their products, but rather people socializing about current events, sports, activities, and a wide variety of subjects.

Remember, the world does not revolve around your business. So don't try to make it the focal point of every conversation you have.

Finally, and most importantly, you always want to provide value to your social network friends and connections. If you find an article or video that holds value for you, chances are it will hold value for many of your connections as well. After all, your network is mainly comprised of people who share similar interests. The more value you provide, the more people are going to grow to know you, trust you, and, over time, want to do business with you.

Despite the popularity, ease of use, and fun of Internet social networking, it's also important to network in your community as well. Joining entrepreneur groups, referral clubs, and attending chamber and networking events will never go out of style, regardless of how much momentum Twitter, Facebook, and the others continue to gain. Getting to know other business owners in your area through the aforementioned methods can give your business a tremendous boost and build your network even more so.

I am an Internet Marketing consultant and business coach who assists you in launching and operating a successful home-based business. My team and I have helped countless individuals generate five, even six-figure income streams from the comfort of their home. Discover my full story! Visit WhoIsJasonCercone.com

Jason Cercone

The Role of Social Networking in Marketing

During the 2008 presidential election season, social networking sites were used for the first time by major candidates. Barack Obama's campaign successfully used sites such as Twitter and Facebook to add to his appeal with younger voters and to spread his message more quickly, easily and inexpensively. Indeed, social networking sites proved their mettle during that election season, and businesses who underestimated their value quickly learned how important they can really be.

Obama's campaign used these different sites in different ways. On Twitter, people were able to "follow" Barack Obama. This created a sense of belonging to his campaign, and made his fans and supporters feel as if they were somehow actually connected to the candidate. In turn, the Obama campaign would "follow" different people in order to return the favor and encourage them to read the messages they sent out.

The way that Obama's campaign used Twitter to send messages and updates to its supporters is a great example of how a business can take advantage of this powerful site. Obama's Twitter profile was always active; it sent out dozens of "tweets" per day. Likewise, a business can drum up a lot of support and excitement, but it needs to maintain an active Twitter account and continuously send out updates to its followers.

Another powerful tool used during the 2008 election by the Obama campaign was Facebook. Facebook saw a massive explosion in its membership numbers during the year 2008, and Obama took full advantage of this fact. Once reserved for young people attending school, Facebook is now open to people of all ages - and they generally begin logging in on a routine basis. Knowing this, Obama's campaign created a very visible Facebook presence and quickly befriended thousands of Facebook users.

A business can easily do the same basic thing that Obama did using Facebook. Creating a business presence on the site is easy to do; gathering up hundreds of friends isn't quite as simple. However, over time a larger group of fans or friends can be acquired. Once it is, people trying to market their business can look to how the Obama campaign used Facebook to its advantage during the election.

On Facebook, the Obama campaign created a feeling of belonging for thousands of its supporters. It created a place for people to meet and discuss the campaign and what they liked about the candidate. In the same way, a business can generate a lot of buzz about their products or services by having a presence on Facebook. People can visit a company's Facebook page to learn more about it, discuss it and generate excitement for it.

From a financial standpoint, social networking sites are a clear marketing winner. They are essentially free; some additional features may cost money, but their overall effect more than pays those fees. They are very versatile and can be adapted to fit just about any marketing strategy. Their ability to reach out to millions of people is very potent, and forward thinking businesses should look to the Obama campaign for inspiration as they look for new marketing techniques.

Jon Reasa

The Seven Deadly Sins of Business Networking (and How to Avoid Them)

The seven deadly sins are transgressions that stymie spiritual progress. But what if these sins were applied to business networking? Follow these tips to make your next networking endeavour a heavenly experience.

Pride - Arrogant or disdainful conduct or treatment; haughtiness . (Source: American Heritage ® Dictionary of the English Language)

This sin has been called the most deadly of all the deadly sins. And for good reason. Whoever has pride has an excessive love of themselves. At a networking event, they tend to ignore people or they ignore your business needs. This person is full of self-importance and will talk endlessly about her products, her services and how happy her clients are with her.

Instead of pride, you should be modest. Talk about yourself, but only after finding out what the other person does for a living. You can be successful by crafting a memorable introduction that you can say in 30-seconds or less. Then, take the time to listen to what the other person has to say.

Greed ; An excessive desire to acquire or possess more than what one needs or deserves, especially with respect to material wealth . (Source: WordNet 2.0, Princeton University)

In business, we all want to do well financially. Yet, when one is greedy, this can impede on our ability to form meaningful relationships. At a networking event, a greedy person is difficult to spot. He tends to ask great questions and praise your expertise in a given area. But what he is doing is picking your brain to understand who 's in your network. He knows what your needs are but is afraid to connect you with the person in his network because he thinks you 're going to steal a great opportunity from him. I call this greedy person a horder.

You can avoid becoming greedy by understanding that networking is all about giving. If you 're generous in what you give to others, you will reap the benefits through increased sales, endless referrals and unlimited job opportunities. So, don 't be afraid to connect people together.

Envy - A feeling of grudging admiration and desire to have something possessed by another . (Source: WordNet 2.0, Princeton University)

Ah envy. Otherwise known as jealousy, or the green-eyed monster. At a networking event, this person resents your achievements, traits, status, abilities or situation. She thinks that you are luckier, more attractive, smarter or better than her. Often, she tends to insult you with a snide remark such as, Oh, you think you 're better than all of us because you sold a company for millions of dollars. Let 's bow down to you. □ She is jealous of your successes.

Don 't fall into this trap. Being envious of someone 's achievements will cause you to resent your own. Instead, list your own business-related successes on a piece of paper. Maybe you just landed a huge account, or maybe you just launched your own business. Whatever your achievements, write them down and share them with the people you network with. Someone may be so impressed with your triumphs, they will hire you for their project.

Wrath - Intense anger; inappropriate (unrighteous) feelings of hatred, or revenge . (Source: American Heritage ® Dictionary of the English Language)

You 've met this person before. He 's angry that the networking event he just paid $20 to attend didn 't produce any clients or immediate sales. Or, he 's angry that a vendor he hired recently for a project not only did a shoddy job, but also has the nerve to show up at the same event as him.

This type of negativity will do more to scare people away than to draw them to you. You should react with kindness when you 're networking. Never badmouth anyone. The business world is a very small world and if you get into a habit of talking bad about anyone, it will come back to haunt you. Instead, if you have a problem with the event you attended, speak directly to the event organizer. Or, if a vendor delivered poor results, pick up the phone and speak to him or her about your unhappiness.

Lust - To have an intense or obsessive desire, especially one that is sexual . (Source: American Heritage ® Dictionary of the English Language)

Business networking is all about gaining new professional contacts. It 's not about asking people out on dates or finding out what their favourite sexual position is. You 'll find this person at every networking event ; she 's too horny to focus on business issues, yet too stupid to realize her mistake. She 'll start asking if you 're married, her eyes will drop down, not only to see the name on your nametag, but to also see if there 's a ring on your finger and she 'll make comments on how gorgeous your smile looks.

When networking, keep your mind out of the gutter by focusing on safe topics. Talk about books you 're reading, the weather, your recent vacation, hobbies you enjoy and goals for your business just so you can keep your mind on godly □ topics.

Gluttony ; The desire to consume more than what one requires. Over indulgence in food or drinks . (Source: Oxford Dictionary)

Who else has met someone who has gotten drunk at a business networking event? I have. He got the free drink ticket at the registration desk, the free drink ticket from the person who admitted she doesn 't drink and found one of the tickets lying on the floor. On top of that, he has bought a few more rounds of suds so he can loosen up. His manners have made a quick exit and he 's louder than the music that 's blaring through the speakers.

Everything needs to be done in moderation, including the consumption of food and drinks at a networking event. Making a first impression is important, but making a lasting impression counts even more. In order to be in control of your mental and physical faculties at an event, stick to just one drink. Better yet, if you go to the event with a buddy, ask him or her to stop you at 1 or 2 drinks. Never attend a networking event hungry. Instead, consume a sandwich or a small salad before you go.

Sloth ; The avoidance of physical work. Idleness, wastefulness, laziness . (Source: American Heritage ® Dictionary of the English Language)

Part of networking is meeting people, but the real work comes from how well you follow up. I 'm amazed at the number of people who collect my business card, promise to call me the next day and I never hear from them again. How rude and inconsiderate, yet many professionals don 't realize that following up means the difference between having a thriving business and just scraping by.

Be enthusiastic when you meet new people and only collect business cards from people who you know you can follow up with. Treat each business card like a $100 bill. This will help you to spend each card wisely. If you find that there 's a mutual benefit to following up with a new business contact, do so no more than 24-hours after meeting him or her. Doing so ensures that the person remembers who you are.

Remember the networking virtues of modesty, generosity, sharing, kindness, humility, moderation and enthusiasm when you work a room. You will gain a reputation for your networking graces and not be remembered for your networking sins.

Leesa Barnes, The Schmooze Coach, helps consultants, virtual assistants, professional organizers, coaches and solopreneurs avoid cold calling by developing a fearless networking plan. Leesa is author of "Schmooze Your Way to Success: 9 Fearless Networking Tips for the Shy, Timid, Introverted & Just Plain Clueless." Go to http://www.schmoozeyourwaytosuccess.com/ecourse.html and sign up for her free 8-lesson ecourse called "From Clueless to Fearless: Secrets from the Schmooze Coach."

Leesa Barnes

The Three Things a Job Seeker Must Know to Use Social Networking As a Job Search Tool

Social Networking (Web 2.0)

The buzz about it is unbelievable. Are you wondering why? It's because using social networking can be the key to your positioning yourself as an expert in your field. By blogging or using sites like Facebook, YouTube, LinkedIn and Twitter, you can reach hundreds or even thousands of people that you never would have had access to otherwise.

If you are in a search for more meaningful work, how can you use these sites in your job search? I must admit I have been asking myself that question quite a bit. I don't pretend to be an expert at these sites as yet but I do have three suggestions that will insure that you get off to a good start.

Is it right for you and your job search?

First take some time to see where social networking fits into your search for more meaningful work and your job search plan. Are you going to add one more networking techniques to your current mix of networking options?

It takes time to get to know the basics of the different social networking sites. You can't just dabble in social networking and expect results. It requires a time commitment. Do you have the time to consistently spend an hour or so a day investigating the various sites, reading up on the sites you are interested in and then trying one or two out?

Give to Get

You might have already noticed that in general self promotion is frowned on in social networking and the web in general. A social network provides a place for people to get to know you. The way that you do that is by giving them something of value - a tip, a quote, an idea, news etc.

What is your Strategy?

So now if after considering it you decide that social networking is for you, then you'll want to make sure you have a strategy and focus. Do the people you are targeting use social networking? Your target could be employers, employees of your target companies, or people doing the kind of meaningful work you have an interest in. How will you get your targets to find you and once they do, what do you want them to do and how will you know they have done it?

As an example I have been using Twitter to announce the publication of my newsletters. I use my newsletters to attract people interested in finding work that is more meaningful. I can see by my web statistics that more people are reading my newsletter online and signing up for it since I began to do that. Is it worth it? Since my newsletter list host automatically notifies Twitter, I spend no extra time doing it. The additional readers are definitely worth it to me.

You must decide for yourself what your strategy is and what result you want. When choosing an action, always consider the time and/or money involved and the impact (result) you expect.

Does it fit your brand?

The third step is to remember your personal brand or image and make sure that there is nothing you do in social networking that inadvertently discredits or changes that image. This is extremely important. Ask yourself, "Does this picture or message enhance or detract from my brand?" Unless your messages are consistent with your brand and image, you will confuse or worse alienate your target.

Most of us started with these various sites because friends invited us to join them. Now may be the right time to give social networking a more serious focus. If so devote the time you need to decide if it is right for you and your market, develop a strategy, and make your messages consistent with your brand.

Take action

1. Comment on blogs - One good way to get started with blogs is to read and comment on other people's blogs. You can establish a name for yourself that way as well.

2. Put your toe in the water. A LinkedIn profile is easy to set up and worth the effort for a job hunter. Take the time to complete the profile in detail. Recruiters and hiring managers often search LinkedIn for candidates for jobs.

3. Got a list? There are many social networks besides Twitter, Facebook and LinkedIn. These are three that are generally accepted for business. There may be others specific to your job or industry. Do a Google search to find them.

Alvah Parker is a Practice Advisor (The Attorneys' Coach) and a Career Changers' Coach as well as publisher of Parker's Points , an email tip list and Road to Success , an ezine. Subscribe now to these free monthly publications at her website http://www.asparker.com/samples.html

Parker's Value Program © enables her clients to find their own way to work that is more fulfilling and profitable. Her clients are attorneys and people in transition who want to find work that is in line with their own life purpose. Alvah is found on the web at http://www.asparker.com She may also be reached at 781-598-0388.

Alvah Parker

The Up and Coming Small Business Trend for 2006 - Teleconferencing Networking

According to the U.S. Business Administration in 2003 of the 5.7 million American businesses, 99% are considered to be small businesses with less than 500 employees. Small business owners continue to grow at a phenomenal rate.

Many business strategies are employed to grow sales including: Search Engine Marketing, Internet Marketing such as online newsletters and traditional marketing such as radio, television and print. Another popular marketing strategy is business to business (B2B) networking through numerous vehicles such as Chambers of Commerce, formal networking organizations and professional associates.

However, in 2006 a new trend emerged. Business networking experienced a complete transformation through the concept of teleconferencing networking . This type of online networking was very new.

One of the earliest companies who offered this type of networking was Fast Pitch Networking. This innovative company developed networking teleconference sessions where you had just 5 minutes to "pitch" what you do to 25 other prospects.

Just think about the advantages that this type of networking provides the small business owner:

Geographic flexibility -- If you have numerous locations or wish to expand to a new market, you can telephone into a conference and share what you do with others no matter where you are at that moment. Reduced costs -- No costs for driving, parking to that weekly or monthly meeting. Also, there is no annual commitment as each meeting has a flat cost. Yes, there is a telephone charge, but many small business owners have flat long distance fees.

More time -- Since you can network from your office or home, you now have more time for additional appointments. You don't have to allow additional time for traffic, road conditions, etc. Convenience -- If you live in the northern states, you can avoid winter's bad weather since you are calling from your office. Again, you attend when you can and pay for only those meetings that you attend. Additional Opportunities - You will have fresh individuals to connect with instead of the same faces that you see weekly or monthly who still haven't become customers. Focus -- In traditional networking environments, there are always distractions from people interruptions to food being served. With online networking or teleconferencing networking, the focus is on you. Now is YOUR time to shine. If you are a small business owner who is an excellent communicator, has developed a strong "Elevator" speech and can quickly establish a rapport using online technology, then on-line networking can only catapult your business to that next level. Watch for this up and coming small business trend in 2006.

How are your other sales skills? Check out this free sales skills assessment

Are you where you want to be? M.A.P. for Success may help you chart a new course for success at http://www.processspecialist.com/action-plan.htm

Leanne Hoagland-Smith

Three Reasons Networking Events Increase Your Referral Business

As every entrepreneur knows, referrals are the lifeblood of small business. Events hosted by professional associations, college alumni groups and your local chamber of commerce are the perfect opportunity to expand your network of professional contacts. Networking leads to a direct increase in the number of referrals you receive for new customers, earning you new business. Yet as a business coach, I've learned that small business owners rarely take the time to attend networking functions.

There are three key reasons that networking for referrals makes good business sense-especially for entrepreneurs:

1. Referrals come to you pre-sold.

When a network contact sends you a referral, they've already done a good part of the selling for you. This is a fantastic concept if you don't enjoy prospecting for new business. With every networking event you attend, have a goal of meeting new people whose business contacts complement yours. With a robust network, you've got your own pro-bono sales force enthusiastically working for you seven days a week. You couldn't build a better sales team than that!

2. Trust is built faster with a referred client.

A key buying motivation with every consumer is reducing risk. No one wants to feel they've made a poor buying decision. A prospect who has been referred to you sees you as a friend of a friend, so you are instantly viewed as trustworthy. A referred customer feels more comfortable during the buying process and tends to purchase more.

The social aspect of networking events is designed to build trust and friendships among business contacts. When attending functions look for ways to assist others in their business-growth objectives, and you'll find yourself surrounded by professionals eager to send business your way as well.

3. Referrals clone more referrals

For long-term revenue growth, nothing beats the multiplying effect of referrals bringing new business directly to you. Your reputation for quality and integrity grows with each new "generation" of referred business. The loyalty factor helps protect you against the fads and gimmicks of your competitors.

Remember that each new referred client has their own circle of influence that represents a whole new door of networking opportunities for you. Find out what professional or social groups your new clients are involved in and offer to provide a short seminar, presentation, or article content for its newsletter. Your valuable insight will win you the enviable reputation of "expert in your field" within that group. And when they need assistance, you'll be the one they call.

The time you spend building relationships within your professional network pays off better in long-term revenue growth than any other marketing strategy. Instead of thinking of networking events as a chore, think of them as a chance to put more money in your pocket. The old adage, "Work smarter, not harder," certainly applies when it comes to networking.

To find great networking opportunities, keep an eye on the schedules published by your local professional association, chamber of commerce and business newspapers. Once you are at an event talk to as many people as possible about your business; it may surprise you how often they need your services or know someone else who does. Dedicate time each week to meet with others in networking activities, and you'll see your referral business grow in ways you never thought possible.

Deborah Walker, veteran coach and revenue building expert helps entrepreneurs and small business owners to improve sales, revenue and profits. Her long-term experience as small business owner provides insight on avoiding the pitfalls of starting, growing and maintaining a small business enterprise. To learn more about revenue coaching visit http://www.RevenueQueen.com

Deborah Walker

Tips On How To Drive Traffic With Bebo - Social Networking With Bebo In Order To Drive Traffic

Bebo is a really cool social site. You need to pick your topic and dive right in. The community, like a lot of social sites is made up of all ages but predominantly teens and early twenty something folks. If your target market fits this demographics then you will be right at home figuring out how to drive traffic with bebo.

Traffic from Bebo is no different that any other social site, I mean, you need to follow the etiquette of the site. That is the first rule. One should never barge into a social site and start to do blatant advertising, this will get you punted from the site permanently.

The key is to become part of the community by sharing information and asking questions. People love to help others and helping you will build bonds with others. You, in return, should be looking at questions others are asking and look up the answers on Google or your favorite search engine. You should never just guess at an answer, since your primary goal is to be perceived as an expert in your field.

As you go about answering questions other people have on your topic, you will start to be perceived as the expert of the group. This will build trust and help bond you to the other folks in the community. These folks will naturally start to follow your site links and recommend them to others. This will start to build traffic and create a social buzz about you and your site.

This in turn will be picked up by Google and give your site higher rankings because of the backlinks being developed on the social site. The social site usually has a high PR and this PR will be pointing toward your site! This is very cool since it helps your site and sales the most. I mean, who does not want more traffic to their site and more sales?

All this snowballs into higher traffic from the social network and the natural search engine results. This will be very targeted traffic which means more sales for you. This is how to drive traffic with bebo. Yes, it is worth the effort. As you will find out, all this buzz about your site will grow and last for a long time. The search engine rankings will not diminish anytime soon either. It is Win-Win-Win all the way around. You help others, others help you, you get more traffic and sales and Google gets a popular site to offer it's clients.

Stop losing money by missing out on the most popular social marketing methods and techniques by visiting http://www.netsensesocialcommunitysecrets.com/ - Your guide to profiting from social networks to include Facebook, Yahoo Answers, Myspace, Bebo and much more!

Tim Gorman

Tips To Help When Attending Networking Events

Useful things to remember when you 're attending networking events.

Network events can fill some of us with dread and fear but bear in mind these thoughts and the whole thing can become a useful business exercise and perhaps even pleasant! For more information about networking events and how to maximise your business skills visit www.exceptionalthinking.co.uk

1. You are about to give up a couple of precious hours, so aim to get the most out of it

2. Get positive and aim to enjoy this event and have some real fun

3. You will see people on their own, open 2 "s and 3 's. They will be welcoming. Beware of the closed 2 's 3 's and 4+ groups unless there are people in there you already know.

4. Get yourself in the right state. AND NOT A RIGHT STATE ☐ Walk in, head held high, shoulders back and smile.

5. Try to think what you have in common with the people at the event? You all travelled to get here; you are guests of the same hosts; you are all here to learn something; you are all in business.

6. Plan to talk to 3 new people and gain 3 new pieces of information.

7. You are not only selling yourself, but also your company, it 's services or products. You are the human face of your organisation. Whatever impression you make, it will be remembered. Make sure it 's a positive one. When somebody has a need for the services you offer you are aiming for people to remember YOU.

8. Approach groups you feel comfortable with. Male/female? Younger /older? Tall/ not so tall? This will help to increase your confidence before you tackle the other groups.

9. You are a decent, hardworking and likeable person. Believe in yourself and in your area of knowledge and expertise

10. Allow the other person to talk and they should do the same for you. Be a good listener.

11. It is more preferable to be more interested than interesting. You learn as much from talking as you do from listening

12. It might happen, but very occasionally you might get rejected. These people aren 't worth giving a second thought to. Let 's focus on the 99.9% of pleasant and welcoming people

13. If you are shy (or believe you are) aim to go with someone you know and "hunt in pairs '. When you find it starts to get easier you can attend the next event on your own.

14. Move on from groups if you are not part of the conversation. Excuse yourself and approach a different group.

15. Everyone at the event wants to network. They want to meet you just as much as you want to meet them.

16. There will be the odd rude person just get away from them as soon as possible

17. Small talk is the foundation of all relationships, even business relationships. All information is useful

18. When you talk business ascertain the person 's background, how business is at present and where they see things going

19. When you ask for a business card always ask permission to call a few days later. Write down the agreed date on the back of their card

20. As soon as you get home diarise the call and annotate all useful information on the card in preparation of making that vital follow up call

Helen Dowling from http://www.Exceptionalthinking.co.uk is a specialist in niche marketing and business plans.

Helen Dowling

Top 3 Fun Networking Questions

A great way to connect and follow up with business professionals at networking events is to engage in great conversations. It is important for professionals to be good talkers as well as good listeners. They should also pay attention to details-small or large. It is also an advantage for business people to remember their colleagues names and professions. An excellent way to build these abilities it to ask fun questions that are memorable and exciting. Asking these type of questions can give professionals insight into their counterparts personalities, likes, dislikes, abilities, strengths and weaknesses.

Here are a few questions below to get the networking ball rolling!

Fun Question #1

If you could be a superhero, who would you be and why?

This question is a great icebreaker and definitely creative. Besides going down memory lane, professionals will have to think hard about who they would select to be. The character whom they choose can say a lot about their ambitions. Their superhero could exemplify how they would like to be viewed or revered in their workplace. Their superhero abilities could be a link to their strengths and talents as well as how they communicate or interact with others. And their superhero choice could mirror their stronger personality traits.

Fun Question #2

Which tv show or movie is similar to your present day life?

This question will definitely stir up a great dialogue and conversation. Learning about what people like to watch in their free time tells a lot about what they value in their social lives. Comedies, mysteries, suspense, drama are all different types of themes that can express the social aspects of many professionals. The tv show or movie can also display a particular actor or character that the professional wishes to emulate. Also pay attention to the theme or moral of the show or movie to find out how the professional views their life and relationship with others.

Fun Question #3

What is your favorite beverage (alcoholic or non-alcoholic)?

This question is great for finding out what tastes do people prefer. Their drink selections could mirror their taste to music, clothes or even cars. It can tell a lot about their personalities and character traits including how they interact with others. Their drink selection can also tell a little about their background or different places where they go for leisure or social fun.

Chi Chi Okezie is owner/producer of SIMPLEnetworking, LLC in Metro-Atlanta, GA. Newly published author of "SIMPLEnetworking: Creating Opportunities ... The new form of success!" View excerpts of the book and polish your professional approach: http://www.snseminars.com

Chi Chi Okezie

Twitter Networking - 5 Essential Tips to Improve Your Twitter Networking and Grow Your Business

As a business owner, or just as someone who is seeking to connect with others in your market, Twitter is truly an incredible medium that can help your networking efforts tremendously. However, there are right and wrong ways of using Twitter for networking. In this article, I will give you 5 important tips on how to network on Twitter properly so that you can get the results you want.

1. Establish exactly what you are trying to achieve with Twitter first. If it's to have a laugh, chat randomly to complete strangers, be excited about others having a laugh as well about random news, go ahead and do this. But this is not the way to achieve business success through networking on Twitter. Therefore, decide exactly what market you are in, what niche you want to represent on Twitter.

This is important because now you can position yourself as an expert in that particular field, which attracts those that need that expert.

2. Build your Twitter profile presence so that people know what you are about. Use your Twitter profile to tell new potential Twitter followers who you are, what your interests are or what your niche is. Let them know what you hope to offer, and even that you are looking for like-minded people to work with, share knowledge with, or do projects with in the future, if that is what you want. Aim to come across friendly, accessible and valuable.

3. Bring value to the table! Offer people opportunities to network with you, to do joint projects. Ask for help, but perhaps more importantly, offer help. When you offer tips, ideas, news etc. about topics that others are interested in, you're Twitter networking will improve a great deal as people will start to see you and a knowledgeable and helpful person they might want to do business with. It will of course also lead to better quality long-term followers.

4. Engage directly with specific Twitterers who you consider people you want to network with. I guess this can be called 'Targeted Twitter Networking'. Its similar to point 3 but you should now look for hot Twittere networking prospects.

Seek them out using tools such as Tweetdeck or search for related tweets and Twitterers by entering your keyword in the search function on Twitter. Engage with others helpfully and people will see you do this and are more likely to want to connect with you too.

5. Don't use your Twitter account for marketing your links all the time. This is crucial. If you 'offer' a new product or service in every tweet, purely to get Twitter traffic to your sites, you will lose followers and come across as 'just another marketer'. However, if you mix your helpful and engaging tweets with the occasional marketing message, people are more willing to accept this and the response to the offer-tweets might well go up.

This, again, will improve your overall standing as someone people might well want to do business with.

Bonus tip! Add value, of course, but...do it consistently. The amazing thing is that you can actually do this totally on auto-pilot. I have used a system that allows you to send repeated valuable messages, get twitter followers all the time, as many as you want, and grow your twitter list exponentially. It works very well for me. Visit here to read more about this twitter business growth tool: Twitter Traffic On Auto-pilot .

Andy Brooks

Twitter Tweets & Networking For Profits on Internet Teaser Markets

"Who do you follow?" the latest buzz about twitter is the growing trend to increase numbers of followers and friends by joining Twitter Banks (for lack of a better term) and following those who follow you. So, how effective is this?

Followers grow exponentially. Although I'm still following twice as many folks as follow me, what can I say? I love people! The reality is, my list keeps on growing and multiplying. Every time I send out a comment, people who don't know me see me and go on my links. Maybe not everyone, but some do.

For some it's simply popularity. For others it's a matter of connections. For the bulk of the personas who settle into networking twitter, it's a means of getting your name out there, becoming a recognizable source of information, and enjoying the process of networking your business.

How do you twitter?

I comment on what I'm doing - not every minute of the day - but randomly throughout the day, I comment on some specific thing I'm doing. Usually I leave three or four links a day on twitter, to drive traffic to my websites. I also brag on twitter... Yeah!!! Give me credit! I love getting acknowledgment for what I do - those private messages, keep 'em coming baby. That's my encouragement!

How does twitter profit your business?

Recommendations, referrals, recognition and reputable links are all resources of twitter. These powerful messages, sent out to the masses return in targeted visitors to your website and dollars in your bank account. Twitter hasn't replaced word of mouth advertising, it's improved it.

Some famous folks twitter, besides me. I'm sure you'll recognize a few names on the list of twitter occupants once you get there and start signing on followers and folks to follow. There will be a host of new friends come your way, and many you already keep in touch with via other means.

Is this a self promotion? Probably not, of course, I'd be happy to have you follow me. But, more than anything else, this is an invitation to get on twitter and tell the world about your business. Network with friends and family and become involved in a new form of social networking that gives you back a sense of personal communications. Twitter is a step-child to Alexander Graham Bell, that igniter of push-button communications. Only with Twitter, you say what you want to whoever reads your words, whenever they get around to doing it. There's no ringing phone to contend with... unless you twitter to your cellular.

If you're still not twittering... What's stopping you?

Add me to your twitter list at http://twitter.com/janverhoeff and let's be tweet friends.

Jan Verhoeff is an online marketer with a sense of balance, humor and courage. If you're looking for some fun methods of marketing your business online visit http://makeyourfirstmilliononline.com and fill up on ideas, strategies and plans to make a million online.

Jan Verhoeff

Understanding the Basics of Social Networking

Social networking can be a powerful tool for establishing business contacts and building your online profile but are your efforts working for you or are you committing every Facebook faux pas in the book.

The following ten steps won't instantly transform you into an internet marketing whiz but they will point you in the right direction.

Ultimately your success in anything will be dependant on your purpose, ethics and strength of commitment.

If you're out to make a quick buck at someone else's expense, I'm afraid there's no miracle cure for being a dork, but if you are looking to improve your results here's a few tips that will bring some valuable leads and help establish good relationships.

10 - Join Networking Groups

People who join these groups are there to establish networks and contacts. They are happy for you to send them friend requests and share ideas. Facebook has limits on how many friends you can add in a day but there is a way of getting around this.

Many of these groups have lists where you can add your email address to the end of the list. You can then go to your Profile page and go on 'Friends' and select 'Invite Friends'. Down the left hand side there's a link titled 'Invite Friends to join Facebook'.

You simply cut and paste the entire list into this area and it matches it to existing Facebook accounts. By doing it this way, you can send out multiple invites and not get your account suspended and as it's an opt in list, you're not spamming anyone and as the list grows and others join the group, you will continue to receive friend requests.

9 - Take an Interest

As new friends accept your friend requests and send you friend requests, go and have a look at their profiles and look for common interests. Post a 'Thanks for the add,' message on their wall. Keep it simple and polite. Introduce yourself and ask them a question about their interests and take an interest in their response.

8 - Go for Quality over Quantity

Be prepared to cut the dead weight. I think most people have something of value to offer but occasionally you do come across others whose personal value systems conflict with your own or who are going through their Pyramid Scheme phase at the expense of any sort of ethics.

Seek to establish high quality, valuable relationships rather than lots of empty ones. Once a month, use the Pareto Principle (also known as the 80-20 rule) on your networking list. The 80-20 rule means establishing who your top 20% are. Also remember not all valuable contacts are clients or paying customers.

7 - Offer Something of Value

Ensure you are offering something of value and that you don't become a part of other people's 'dodge list'. Be genuine and don't do the hard sell. Offer tips and just be a friend. Remember your manners but don't be too formal or cold. People like establishing relationships with other people with similar interests.

6 - Have a 30 second snapshot of who you are

Underneath your profile picture on Facebook there is a small box where you can say something about who you are and what you represent. If you put something compelling in this box, it will prompt your friends and new associates to read your extended info section and learn more about you. Describe briefly who you are, and what you're about.

5 - Feed the Blog from your Website into your Facebook

You can feed your blog into the 'Notes' section of your Facebook. This will update on your wall and other people's feed and keep your Facebook alive even if you don't log on every day.

To do this go on 'Settings' at the top right of your Facebook Select 'Application Settings' Select 'Profile' On the top left there will be a large blue button that says 'Go to Application' When the new window opens, it will show all your friends notes and there will be a pale blue box on the right with application notes and options. Select "Import Settings" You can then input where the blog feed is coming from - your website or blog.

4 - Send Friend Requests to your favourite Authors and Industry Keynotes

Most authors manage their own Facebooks. Keynotes who are usually inaccessible are seeing the value in establishing an online profile and are usually more than happy to accept your friend requests. In their friend lists, you will find other people who are interested in the same subjects as you. Friend one of two of them and get to know them and swap ideas.

3 - Reply to Status Updates and other People's Notes and Comments

Don't plug yourself or your product. Offer something of value to them, their friends and readers. Compliment other business people on their work when you admire what they are offering. Everyone enjoys positive feedback and if they are using their own Facebook for business also, your feedback will be a valuable testimonial to their potential prospects.

If you have any feedback on potential improvements or disagree with anything, send a private message. It's still good to engage your friends and networks but don't do it publicly if it will affect their reputation or business. Use your good judgement.

2 - Exchange Reviews

If you are an Author or offering a product of service that is complimentary to another persons, an alternative to Pay Per Go and Affiliate promotion is to find someone with a service or product that you would use or do use and post a review on your own website and Facebook. Tag them in the note, and sometimes they will offer to do the same.

You can solicit these relationships but don't overdo it. You want your feedback to be genuine and you don't want to damage your own reputation and become known as someone who plugs everyone and everything. Be selective. If you do include affiliate links in your through text writing, always note that it is an affiliate link. Most people will still be glad to go on the link and give you a kickback in return for your valuable input.

1 - Have a Good Array of Photos

Don't just have the professional shots. Have some family shots or pictures of you doing things you enjoy. Make your Facebook human. Even if you operate two accounts - one for personal contacts and one for professional contacts, include personal photos on each.

People are visual creatures. We retain 70% of what we see.

Logically women's magazines should have men on the covers right? Women are attracted to men, but you rarely see women's magazines with men on the cover and vice versa with men's magazines.

People like looking at images that are similar to themselves. If you are selling a property and include a picture of a woman laughing in the lounge room, it will increase the go through rate. Most of the decision makers in real estate purchases are women. When they are looking at a gallery of 30 images of homes, they will go on the house with the picture of the person in it.

Photographs are a very powerful part of establishing your online identity and something that can make a difference on your success or failure online.

Clearly there's the obvious disclaimer of not posting the drunken shots where you flashed the bartender last weekend, but some photos of you having a couple of quiet drinks with friends and enjoying sports etc do add to your self branding.

If you use your Facebook for networking and business, let your friends know also. Some friends can be a bit loose with their wall posts or tag you in photos you might not want your business associates to see. Always ask your friends to be aware of this when they interact with you via your Facebook.

These are just some of the more useful techniques I've used and found to help me build some strong relationships online. Be yourself and be ethical and you will soon see the results of your efforts.

Written by Tanya Black

AUTHOR: It's Your Life ~Your Adventure ~ Your Choice An entertaining guidebook for managing the crossroads we all face at some point in our lives. 'It's Your Life' draws on business principles to help you decide what you want, why you want it and how to get it and is presented as a series of fun short stories to illustrate the concepts.

Tanya frequently updates her blog and publishes a monthly e-zine "The Paper Doll". Tanya's book can be purchased here .

Tanya M Black

Unfollow - How to Make a Potential Customer Drop You on Social Networking Sites

Social media experts agree to disagree about the proper forms of Tweetiquette and the proper way to interact. Not just on Twitter but on any social network. Sometimes, the mixed opinions are based on the individual's use: is it business, personal or both?

Being that this article is focused around business networking and reaching a potential market and audience, I'm focusing on the business person engaging others on a social network.

Here's the short list of what you can do (and why) in order to ensure that I, as your potential client or customer, will unfollow or unfriend or just give you the boot.

1. Update too much about your breakfast cereal. Yes, I want you to appear human and want to know that there is a person behind the URL you keep sending me but really, how many times you eat corn flakes doesn't interest me. 2. Send me the URL to your business site too many times. Today's count was nineteen times! I like to know what your website is but please, if I haven't gone to it yet, I probably won't. 3. Tweet and update your status too many times. True enough, I want to surround myself with successful people and learn useful, insightful

things but you can only retweet that teleconference you are hosting so much. 4. Don't be truthful on your profile. Please, do tell as to what your purpose is. Why are you here? Is it personal? Business? Are you launching a site? If it is business, please don't misrepresent your intentions by updating your status to show you are watching Cops with your ex after your argument about the kids. 5. Be selfish. Tweet and update only things that pertain to you. I'll perceive you as one sided and won't care what you have to say. Why? Because this is social networking. I want some kind of relationship with you, even if it is nothing but a familiarity with your name and company. If all you do is show concern for yourself and promotion, why would I be interested in doing business with you? What is in it for me? 6. Give me a product pitch in direct messaging. I certainly don't mind being thanked for following or adding someone...actually, it is thoughtful. But please, don't pitch yourself or your product in the same sentence. That's why I look at your profile before I follow you. 7. Look at me as a number. Yes, I bring your following and friend count up; however, if that is all I am to you, then we don't need any kind of relationship. It goes back to quality vs. quantity, count vs. content. 8. Confuse me with all your networks. Twitter is different from Facebook is different from LinkedIn, etc. I might be on one social network but not another. You can use an auto-update application but please make your "post" generic, as I may not understand. 9. Send ninety inspirational quotes. Yes, I like them but there are websites that can provide that for me. Give me something that is unique to YOU and that only YOU can contribute. 10. Use my tweet or update as your own. I love re-tweets, etc. but can you let folks know it wasn't you? Must you really take credit for it? Isn't that stealing?

We're all learning and listening to new information about social networking and how to use it properly. Please, keep in mind that sometimes what you DON'T do is just as important as what you DO. Quality over quantity counts for more than you might realize.

Don't make me unfollow you. Keep me in your network so that I might learn from you, be inspired and perhaps make a purchase, become a client or a referrer to your services. I found something interesting about you and your business, otherwise I wouldn't have started being in your network!

Mary Lanphier is an internet marketing advisor specializing in social networking and integrating web 2.0 in new business launches. As part of a team at Inspired Business Resources led by Christiane Holbrook, the "go to" person for new business launches. You are invited to get your free "Launch With Impact" manual at http://www.inspiredbusinessresources.com/

Mary Lanphier

Use Social Networking For Business

You probably already know that social networking is not only a buzz in the Internet but also a great business idea. Its great because people just keep coming and membership seems to be continuously increasing in that sites. While social networking websites were initially a venue where people can connect with their family and friends, these sites have evolved into a platform where one can gain business contacts and market ones products and services. More and more businesses and marketers are using these social networking sites to spread the word about their business.

Knowing that many people are bound to sign up for membership in a SocNet site, you dont have to dive into building a SocNet business without careful thought. And one of the most important things to plan and ensure is being able to use a reliable dating software that caters to all your needs as a business owner.

You have to use a SocNet software that provides interactivity to your SocNet site. Your social networking site is not just a webpage that can be read by your members; its an interactive platform to help people get connected easily. But you have to be careful in order not to get stuck with just planning for interactivity. This interactivity and all its aspects, after all, have to have a point and have to be useful. If it does not help your members, then revise your plan. You need a dating software or socialNet software that is helpful and of use to your members.

When choosing a socialNet provider, the company you're hiring has to have skilled programmers and makes use of current online trends smartly. They have to be precise about your specific users needs and be able to meet that with their software.

By choosing the right socialNet provider, you can save your time and money by relying on the professional knowledge of experts instead of doing and learning everything on your own. DatingSiteBuilder.com is one such provider. Visit the website or call toll free 1-800-778-1360.

http://www.datingsitebuilder.com

Nico Kurniawan

Use Social Networking Sites to Promote

This article will cover some basic ideas about using social networking sites to promote your business. Social networking sites have been around for quite some times but they have just gained more popularity over the recent years with a few of the most well known being FaceBook and MySpace.

If you are not familiar with a social networking site is, I will quickly explain it here. Simply put these sites are designed for friends to keep in touch or so that people can find new friends of similar interests. When you sign up for the sites, you get a personal profile page where you can post a profile picture and some descriptions about you as well as list interests and such. The profile page can be customized and you can make it really personal. How much the profile can be customized vary on each of the sites.

I mentioned MySpace and FaceBook before since I know that both these sites allow business profile pages. And even though it ´s not necessary to turn your profile page into a sales page, it can be very useful depending on what you are selling or promoting. I've seen people who just use their profile pages to socialize and they talk about the product to their friends and drive traffic to their sales pages that way.

Both of the techniques work and what you decide to go with is really up to you. Maybe you already have a FaceBook and MySpace page but you just didn't use it for this before. However you decide to use these sites, remember to read and follow their rules since each sites rules are different.

What you also should do is to use several social networking sites. You can easily use Wikipedia to find a list of a bunch of networking sites to get you started. Apart from the ones I've mentioned here (facebook.com and myspace.com) I will also mention Yuwie, since Yuwie is a social networking site with all the regular features, but with the added perk of getting payed to use it. Because of this feature, Yuwie seems to attract a lot of people working online or being interested in working online, which might give you a pre-targeted market already (again, depending on what you're promoting).

When you've signed up for a number of social bookmarking sites it ´s time to start designing your profile. Make your profile eye catching and nice looking, don't just plaster your profile with banners and links to the things you are promoting because that will just make it look bad and not very personal. Try to make the profile page sell by showing how the product helped you, if possible. And use the social networking sites for what they are, make friends.

Apart from being a good source of possible customers or such, you can also make good connections to people who work online and you might find new friends to learn from and share ideas with. And as a bonus, the social networking sites are also quite fun.

If you would like to read more articles related to making money online, head over to http://www.MaverickMoneyMakingHome.com/ where I write about my experience in internet marketing.

Anders Fredricsson

Using Social Networking Sites For Dating

The use of social networking sites for free online dating is on the rise. An increasing number of men and women are turning to networking websites to find dates. They find these websites as reliable sources in finding out the persona of the person and the increasing numbers of options on these websites has enriched user experience and has prompted this trend. Here are the top reasons why dating through socials networking sites gos:

Profile: the profile is getting increasingly longer which means that you get to know the person well even with just one visit to their profile. Their likes and dislikes, past experiences are all detailed out in the profile.

Photographs: all social networking sites come with the option of uploading photographs and videos. You get to see how your date looks and the obscurity that blind dates bring is eliminated.

Groups/communities: each person is a member of one or more community and a look at this speaks volumes about the personality of the person. It is a good way to judge the person.

Friends: every person on a social networking sites would have made a couple of friends you can talk to or at least know through their profiles. This is also a way to judge the nature of the person.

Chat rooms: this is one of the most interesting feature in a community website. most of them have it and you can use the chat option to talk to the person and know the person before venturing a date. By doing this you are most likely to end up dating with the right person since you get to know all you wanted about that person. Most people start off safe as friends and then consider the option of dating the person.

From the discussions above, its clear that dating through social networking sites is a good option and the increasing popularity of this mode of dating is no surprise.

I am a dating enthusiast and I like exploring and reviewing websites for free online dating and singles chat.

Jack Meijer

Using Social Networking Sites To Advance Your Career

Should you accept them all, or try to accept some while ignoring others? Most importantly, how can you nurture these relationships in a beneficial way to advance your career?

For most part, the rules in the real world should work in the virtual world, too. For social networking sites, it is important to follow up on the contacts that you have built.

Easy Networking

Though networking sites make it easy to connect with different people, adding contacts on your online networking site is only the first step in effective networking. It is just like getting a business card at a formal party - you have to follow up and keep in touch with your contacts.

Making valuable contacts and then letting them drop is one of the biggest mistakes that you can make.

Maintaining Identities

If you prefer that your boss doesn't find out about several aspects of your personal life, then it is possible and preferable that you separate your work life from your virtual personal life. This can be done on almost any of the social networking sites today.

You can let your boss know that you are setting up a dedicated page for professional contacts, and can ask him to be added as a friend there. This should be done in a gracious manner, but you should take care to keep this page separate from your personal page.

Invitations and Recommendations

At times, you might receive an invitation from someone you don't really relate to. It is not necessary to reject them right away - this could be seen as being rude. You can accept the invitation, but take no further action. You do not need to endorse that particular person.

You should use social networking sites to strengthen ties with your business associates by garnering recommendations from them, and by posting referrals for them.

Confidentiality

Always know your company's policy. You don't want to post or mention something on the site that is a company secret without realizing it. Many companies conduct searches on the Internet and monitor blog posts, so always take care with what you post online. Nothing meant for internal correspondence or anything that your company believes can harm their business prospects should be visible on your networking page.

Apart from this, you should also be extremely careful when posting pictures online. No photos that might show you in an embarrassing situation, or relating to nudity or drug use should be posted on your networking page. You should also refrain from posting material that may be politically incorrect.

Your idea is to increase your business prospects, and not make personality statements. Stick to your goal when using social networking sites, and your career will benefit.

Tony Jacowski is a quality analyst for The MBA Journal. Aveta Solutions - Six Sigma Online (http://www.sixsigmaonline.org) offers online six sigma training and certification classes for six sigma professionals including, lean six sigma, black belts, green belts, and yellow belts.

Tony Jacowski

Using Social Networking to Boost Your Online Sales

Promotion is vital in any business, even to those that are being done online. The entrepreneur should make use of different ways to advertise his business effectively. Some strategies are cost effective and it's worth knowing what they are.

Long ago, the advertisement trend is promoting products with the use of the radio and television. Other promotional strategies were composed of giving away of flyers and sending mails. Nowadays, business strategies were updated and entrepreneurs find advertising on the net as a very effective way in making their businesses known. However, there are ways that are totally free and you only need to invest time. One example of these ways is joining a social networking website.

Popular social networking sites include Facebook, Twitter, MySpace and others. Before, only people who want to meet new friends, particularly teenagers and stay-at-home moms, use these sites. They blog about what they are experiencing in life. They talk about their families and love life. They post stuffs just for the sake of sharing a piece of themselves to the other social networkers.

Nowadays, online entrepreneurs found out that they can also be great tools to promote their products and services. By connecting with people, the chance of becoming known becomes bigger. Businesses in different parts of the world are now benefiting from this strategy. This tool will help you attract more customers without having to pay for anything. You only need to register on different websites and start doing the task.

First and foremost, you can create a group which where you can reach people who would be interested in what you are offering. Make it an open group where everyone is welcome to join. By doing this, you will make the group grow with less effort because your friends on that social site will be inviting their friends to join. You can also make use of the discussion area of that group where in you will let the group members interact with each other.

Make it a point also to update your profile by posting whatever is new on your business. If your business has a new campaign or launches a new product, you can post it on the social networking so that everyone there will get the chance to know about it, particularly your friends.

Most of these sites have forums. You can join in the discussions or create your own threads. Attach your signature. It will appear at the bottom of every post that you will place in the forum. Whenever visitors and participants in that forum go on your signature, they will be redirected to your website; thus, they will know more about your business.

As an entrepreneur, you would be surprised to know that most of your business rivals are already into social networking. This is because they want to strengthen their presence on the internet. It will serve you best if you will also join this bandwagon. You won't just be known, you will also establish your credibility while winning more and more customers each day. What's even better is that you will be able to promote yourself in an enjoyable way.

Patrick is a passionate believer in the power of technology to better the lives of everyone and his passion and drive are hallmarks of his attitude to doing business.

Check out more about him @ http://onlinewebmarketingtips.com for more Online Web Marketing Tips and Know more about ways to earn income online at http://www.internetbusinessmodelonline.com

Patrick Sia

Ways to Increase Business With Social Networking Websites

Social networking sites grant assorted humans to commune with one another and share data. The social network is occupied with humans and connections that associates them jointly. It can be a grouping of class members distributed around the area, to regimes and even professional groupings. Here are a few of the methods that you will be able to benefit by utilizing social networking sites.

Social networking provides a lot of people to communicate, and among the most red-hot ways of advertizing is through with the word of mouth. Whenever one person grants some other a fine review of your site, merchandise or service, this 2nd individual successively might stop by to visit your web site. By getting engaged with electronic networks that are have related interests as your merchandise provides is that you will be able to use this social media communication to your reward.

The hard function of social networking is retrieving the sites that provide to your interests that will all the same allow you to create profit from. Choose a matter that is excessively liberal, and you are certain to get a lot of competitors. Pick out one that is excessively constrictive, and you will not hold a tolerant enough client base to profit on. You require to determine the balance of exclusivity and fame.

Social sites are as well a distinguished home to detect novel possible customers. Discovering the correct clients for your merchandise or service is one-half of the combat of advertising your merchandise. As people that have corresponding interests incline to stick together, but might function in dissimilar interest sets. You will be able to exercise this to your reward in two methods - one, you already have a core group of possible customers to begin on. In addition, if they feel liking your merchandises or services, they'll share with acquaintances in additional circles in addition to, building up your orbit of work as if rippling on a pool.

Social networking sites as well grant your clients to develop the belief that they are in contact with you - and masses lean to purchase items from people that they acknowledge or that they are comfier with. So to apply this most effectively, you have to be an outstanding character on the social network web site. Be a participating poster in fine standing and continue your name as among the leaders of the grouping.

By similar lines, you have to recollect that the most eminent social networking relationships are long. If you need your social networking to be efficient, you require to germinate durable friendly relationships with the masses in your social networking groups.

Are you a newbie or have been really doing well on social networking websites? Willing to expand your contacts with friends, family and associates? Visit Pikatcho Online Community . Easy to sign-up and catch up with your new and old associates. Try now!

Michael Corbin

Web 2.0 & Social Networking Etiquette - Social Network Marketing in 2009!

I am so pumped to have finally discovered someone who understands social networking etiquette and how it will be effective in marketing on social networking sites in 2009! Further he explains it is simple terms. I kick myself for not realizing the simplicity of this earlier in my career. If I had, who knows how much further in the game I would be now.

So many people on sites like Facebook, Twitter, MySpace, etc are networking in the worst way imaginable - and they wonder why their online business isn't growing. They're out there blatantly spouting their business plan and opportunity to as many people as possible in as short of time as possible. What they don't realize, is that they are in effect Spamming the entire community of networkers they are trying to attract.

You should be treating your connections and friends in all of these social networking sites like people you're meeting for the first time. Imagine being at a dinner party, someone comes up and introduces themselves, and says something like "Hi, my name is Joe-Bob Smith...Do you want to join my online business opportunity?" You'd have to be thinking to yourself, "Come on!! Is this guy really serious?" Well guess what folks, if you're leading with your online opportunity first when you meet someone online in a social network, that's exactly how it's coming across. A blatant sales pitch!

And then they're left wondering why they have no leads coming in from those sites they're networking in. If you haven't seen this video yet about the social networking etiquette, check out this video by Perry Belcher - the guru of social networking. Social networking is going to be a HOT topic in 2009, so now is the time to start learning how to do it properly.

Enjoy the video - http://www.youtube.com/watch?v=zn1cspHx7DU&feature=channel page

Learn Something Today! - Linus Ruzicka

http://www.mlmprospectformula.com

My name is Linus Ruzicka and I'm an Internet Marketer. I find fulfillment in sharing strategies, tools, tips, and techniques to help other internet and network marketers develop the success they know is attainable online, but just haven't gotten there yet. Trust me, it is possible, but this will not come easily. See, there is still work to be done on your part. Thousands of others are pitching their opportunity and their products. This is not an easy task as you may know. But, when YOU arm yourself with the training that enables you to know how to professionally market yourself instead of your opportunity, then you will find yourself heads and shoulders above the masses of other networkers pitching their opportunity and business. You will be attracting leads to you instead of you hunting for them.

What is the true value of knowledge when you don't put it to use?

Linus Ruzicka

Linus Ruzicka

What is Networking and Why Do We Need This Simple, Fundamental Business Skill

Networking is a fundamental business and life skill. It is the ongoing process of building and developing an interconnected web of mutually beneficial relationships. In other words, you meet people and build some kind of relationship with them, whether it's a deep friendship or occasional business contact. You strengthen relationships by communicating with people, providing them with things they need, finding common interests, and doing things together. The relationship is cemented when the other person finds a way to help you in the form of information, support, or business referrals. It is a cycle of actions, interactions, and follow-up.

As you repeat this process with more and more people, you will have an ever-expanding pool of contacts that you know, have done things for, and can count on them to help you in return. You will be at different stages with different people. Relationships will grow stronger, wane and perhaps end, but an experienced networker will have a net growth in their base of close "friends" and in the sheer number of people they have interacted with.

Not every contact will be a friend, but most of them should be friendly. You may have members of your network who you are not friends with and may not even like, but because you have done something for them, they are willing to reciprocate. The tie will be stronge and more reliable if you have a personal relationship. A non-friendly relationship is only there as long as you can do something for each other.

This process is called "networking". The result of it is your "network", a group of people you have some level of reciprocal relationship with.

It's a very simple series of activities. Go places, meet people, interact with them, and keep track of who, what, where when. That's it. Simple stuff. So why is it so hard for us to start networking or to do it consistently? Because it's easy to not do. Today's business environment is complicated and our daily lives are over-booked, over-stressed, and over-analysed. We find ourselves resisting networking because we are overwhelmed. We've overthought the process until it seems like a hopeless complication, not a vital activity that will benefit us now and will compound over time.

If we return to the foundation of networking - a simple process of building relationships - we'll find ourselves more willing to get started and keep going. Take a few minutes each day to find a way to take simple step forward in any relationship you currently have. Find a way to expand your current contacts just one person at a time. By not overwhelming ourselves with a complicated process, we can grow our network and build our businesses.

Beth Bridges is the Membership Director of the Clovis Chamber of Commerce in California. She has helped thousands of people get connected through hundreds of networking events with the Chamber and other organizations. Learn more about the Clovis Chamber at http://www.clovischamber.com and read Beth's blog at http://bethbridges.blogspot.com which takes a look at networking from the perspective of someone who's met thousands of networkers - good and bad.

Beth Bridges

What is Social Networking?

Have you been asking yourself, what is social networking? Social networking is done by using the many social groups out there as a media for marketing your business. This type of marketing is one of the fastest growing and least expensive methods of reaching potential customers. Many companies and small businesses have found that by using this type of marketing they have been able to brand themselves like never before.

Let's take a look at some of the social sites and after you try it you may find out that it is a lot of fun as well.

Facebook - Facebook was originally launched in 2004 and is open to anybody thirteen and over. Facebook was originally intended for use by college students but opened up to everybody in 2006. Since 2006, Facebook has been growing steadily becoming one of the largest social networks on the internet. One of its close competitors, MySpace, has been loosing momentum while Facebook continues to grow with leaps and bounds.

Twitter - Twitter is the newest of the social sites and has become internationally famous thanks to the many celebrities who like to talk about their daily activities. You may recall the Tweet competition that Ashton Kutcher had with CNN. Twitter has become a daily ritual for many users and due to its rapid growth many techniques have been implemented to make money from its use.

Twitter users send out," Tweets", which is kind of like sending out a short instant message. Its short messaging platform has people from all walks of life sending out their tweets on a daily basis for personal and business use. An example of a business use would be to send out a Tweet when you make a new post to your blog. Your followers will then be able to see what you have been working on and pay a visit to your new post which hopefully you have linked to your main website. But as always, the quality of your posts should be first with quantity being second.

MySpace - MySpace was started in 2003 to compete with other social sites like Friendster. MySpace continues to have a loyal following of users who want to keep in touch with friends and family. Setting up a profile is relatively easy with the step by step instructions that are given when you sign up. During setup you can add photos, school information and even your business information. During the last year or so, MySpace has lost some of its edge due to the growing popularity of Facebook and Twitter but it continues to be a site worth looking in to.

From an internet marketing standpoint, social networking can be as productive as placing ads on websites and will be a lot easier on your wallet. Using Facebook, Twitter and MySpace to market your business will allow a whole new audience to see what you have to offer. Take this opportunity to brand yourself with a lot of unique and useful content and watch your internet business grow. Good luck and best wishes, Tim Stokes.

The author, Tim Stokes, has several ways for you to make money at the Affiliate Earning Website . Visit today and get started with your own home based business.

Tim O Stokes

What is Your Networking Quotient?

Use these 10 questions to determine how focused you are on Networking

1. I have at least 400 people in my network who receive information from me at least once a month

2. I have a compelling 30-second commercial

3. I focus more on selling through my relationships than on selling to people directly

4. I have marketing materials like business cards, brochures and a website, which showcase my expertise. They have a clear, attention getting headline, bulleted points about what I can do for my clients and a low risk, irresistible offer

5. I ask more questions than talk and take time to get to know the people I meet

6. I have a list of top ten referral partners

7. I meet at least one new referral partner a week

8. I thank my referral partners using note cards, gifts and reciprocal referrals

9. Within 2 business days I call and talk to the referral provided to me by a referral partner

10. I practice win-win philosophy both in business and personal life

So how did you do? If you got 10 out of 10, obviously you are a professional networker. On the other hand, if your score is below 7, you have not tapped into your network effectively enough. Either you have not been focused enough on building your network or you have not learned the skills in getting the most out of your network.

There are three keys to networking:

a. The size of your network: The bigger the network, the better it is.

b. The influence of people in your network: Very few sales professionals and business owners pay attention to this part. They don't realize that it is better to have a handful of influential people in your network than a number of people with very little influence. The other part is how influential are these people in your target market. Some people are influential but have very little to do with your target market. Make sure the people you are networking with have credibility and access to your target market.

c. Your skill in influencing your network: Again most people assume that they have the necessary skills. All they have to do is show up at a few events and shake hands. That is the strategy which is based on hope. Also this shows that the salesperson is an amateur networker. The question you must ask is what are you doing consistently to make your network obligated to provide you referrals? Giving gifts, leads and solving people's problems on an ongoing basis is the key to gaining influence in your network.

I hope this has given you a good start in understanding the power of networking and how to go about it.

Download FREE First Two Chapters of "Network Your Way To $100,000 and Beyond" at http://www.networkto100000.com

Minesh Baxi, business coach

877-968-2500

mbaxi.com

minesh@mbaxi.com

Watch 52 video clips and articles from the book "Network Your Way To $100,000 And Beyond" at http://www.NetworkingSeries.com Minesh Baxi and Chuck Gifford are the authors.

Minesh Baxi

What Strengths Do You Have to Offer As a Social Networking Advertising Firm?

If you are a small business, then by now you've probably discovered the need to be online with a website and participate a bit online with your customers in social networks or at least send out coupons by email and newsletters. A busy small business person does not always have time keep up with a blog and all that is required to market and advertise on social online networks.

But luckily there are people that can help and they know all the ropes. You can see where the online exchange of ideas with creative and innovative people could serve your company well, but you do not know where to start. Perhaps, you need to find someone who understands advertising and has strengths within the online social networking realm with regards to Branding and Marketing.

Then ask them for some samples and examples of their successes there? Ask them if they understand the user demographics of online social networks, if they have read the book:

"Go - What Millions of People are Doing Online and Why it Matters" by Bill Tancer; Hyperion, NY - 2008.

If so, ask them what their thoughts on it? If they have studied the social networking game to that extent then you need to see if they can help you design a plan to put your business in front of your target audience online. Review this plan and you may find this venue to be the most inexpensive advertising and marketing you have ever done. This might be a good strategy for you to get through this recession.

Lance Winslow - Lance Winslow's Bio . Lance Winslow is also Founder of the Car Wash Guys, a cool little Franchise Company; http://www.carwashguys.com/history/founder.html/ .

Lance Winslow

What to Do at a Networking Event

Follow these simple steps for making networking a breeze.

1. Choose networking events wisely. Don't waste time attending events that won't serve you. Make a list of your top 5 networking event choices.

2. Research the group and event that you plan to attend so you have talking points and an idea of who else will be there. Keep notes on each event.

3. Get organized - bring your business cards and other helpful materials such as a notebook, pen, etc. What will you include in your networking toolkit?

4. Prepare ahead of time so you know what to wear, what to bring and how long it will take to get there. This way there is no last minute rushing to detract from your confident arrival. Create a pre-event checklist:

a. Is my outfit clean, pressed and ready?

b. Have I done my research?

c. Is my Networking Toolkit complete and in my bag/briefcase?

d. Do I have the correct address, directions and times?

e. How do I feel? (You will feel more confident if you are comfortable and feeling good.)

5. Bring a business card holder, notebook or folder to neatly hold material you collect from others at the event. It looks more professional and it shows respect for the work others have done to create their materials. You're also less likely to lose an important name or number. You can make this a standard part of your Networking Toolkit.

6. Approach valuable contacts (remember quality vs. quantity and Centers of Influence) - it's not a race, talk to people who appeal to you not just as many people as you can. Always begin a conversation with small talk rather than jumping right in to business topics. It's more polite and a much better way to build relationships. What strategies will you use to approach people with whom you would like to become acquainted?

7. Don't push your contact info on people you meet - make them want to ask you for it. This is where having useful information to offer them is helpful. You can also ask if you can contact the person in the future if you feel that they would be open to that. What are some ways you can put the value you have into a tangible article or piece of information that you can share with others? For example, write an article, create a list of resources or an assessment tool you can hand out. Remember to include your contact information on anything you share with others.

8. Debrief your experience of this event after you leave. Take a few minutes to write down some notes or comments about how you felt, who you spoke to, if you feel this was an effective venue for your networking, etc. What did you do or say that worked and what didn't? What are the criteria with which you will assess networking events?

9. Follow up with anyone you promised to contact. Make the calls, send the emails and forward along any material in a timely fashion. This is an extremely important step. If you don't think you will follow through on a promise, don't make one. Not keeping promises will have a negative impact on your personal and professional reputation. Create a simple process for following up with networking contacts. Perhaps you will create a chart that you list networking promises on with a place for checking off completed items. Consider the model below:

10. Stay in touch with the important network contacts you meet consistently as you build your network. For example: you might decide to send a quarterly newsletter on your business to your network or send birthday cards to people in your network. Choose one or a couple of activities that you are comfortable with and do them consistently. How will you maintain contact with your network?

Download Ruth's powerful free confidence building e-book and receive her latest articles at http://www.confidencementor.com/15.html and receive a free subscription to her popular online newsletter, IALAC News (which stands for I Am Lovable And Capable), which brings a weekly dose of practical and powerful confidence to its readers.

As a formerly extremely shy underachiever, Ruth truly understands the personal demons that hold women back and, most importantly, how to shed those demons and become authentically our powerful brilliant selves. Learn more and contact Ruth at http://www.ConfidenceMentor.com

Ruth Hegarty

What You Need to Know About Social Media - Bookmarking and Networking

Although the age of Web 2.0 has come and gone, the sites that marked this period of Internet history - social media sites - are still going strong.

Social media generally refers to one of two thing - bookmarking or networking. Each type of social media offers unique opportunities in terms of search engine marketing.

Social bookmarking sites include Digg, Del.ic.io.us., and Yahoo! Buzz. These sites have basically built on the premise of saving your "favorites" or bookmarking a page you enjoy. Users simply mark a page that they like, and that page is then shared with their contacts on that social bookmarking site. For example, a person reading your article might "Digg it," and your article will then be displayed on their friends' screens as a suggestion. Social bookmarking is an easy way to build inbound links and direct traffic to content on your page.

Social networking, on the other hand, is used to describe community-based sites such as Twitter, Facebook, MySpace and LinkedIn. These sites allow users to find "friends" or "connections" with whom they share messages, photos, videos, links, updates and other information. These virtual networks contribute greatly to the ability of a story, video, song, or other form of media to "go viral" because every person who adds a link to the item automatically shares it with their network. Most websites could benefit from developing a profile on the social networks that cater to their target audience. Social networking is a great way to meet new followers, share information about your product, create inbound links, and generate more traffic to your site.

Discover the secret "Traffic Snowball System" Jason Nyback used to drive over 1,175,000 new visitors to his tiny websites & how you can to - Visit here Now to get access to this free video that reveals all.

To discover proof of how you can drive thousands of visitors to your website using this insider "Can't Miss" system - Visit here Now .

Jason Nyback

Which Social Networking Site is Right For Me?

If you're in commercial real estate this is something you have probably started to ask yourself. Do you immerse yourself and join every possible site out there, automate all your postings with Ping.FM and run the chance of not having the time to manage responses to all these sites or do you select a couple key places to better manage your ability to interact with potential clients on a more personal level?

While the first option may sound great as far as exposure for your listings, advertising on a site that doesn't have your target audience in mind may end up causing you to waste a lot of time on setting up accounts you don't need. While from a business standpoint it may be worthwhile to create the accounts to block others from using the company's name, that's not always a concern when you're focusing on your individual listings. To help in deciding which place may be the best for you to hang your hat I've taken a look at some of the demographic information provided by Quantcast.com on several of the most popular social sites and compared to our typical client information.

The following sites are in order of popularity based on subscriber information and visitor traffic. US Site Views are based on 30-Day increments.

Facebook.com US Site Views: 90.8 M Majority Users: 54% Female Age: 46% are 18 to 34 Income Level: 30% over $100k/yr

MySpace.com US Site Views: 62.7 M Majority Users: 57% Female Age: 46% are 18 to 34 Income Level: 25% over $100k/yr

LinkedIn.com US Site Views: 10.9 M Majority Users: 56% Male Age: 43% are 35 to 49 Income Level: 38% over $100k/yr

Ning.com US Site Views: 7.3 M Majority Users: 54% Female Age: 35% are 35 to 49 Income Level: 16% over $100k/yr

Bebo.com US Site Views: 5.1 M Majority Users: 60% Female Age: 45% are 12 to 17 Income Level: 20% over $100k/yr

Hi5.com US Site Views: 4.0 M Majority Users: 52% Male Age: 48% are 18 to 34 Income Level: 6% over $100k/yr

Friendster.com US Site Views: 1.9 M Majority Users: 52% Male Age: 29% are 35 to 49 Income Level: 27% over $100k/yr

Orkut.com US Site Views: 485.9 K Majority Users: 54% Male Age: 55% are 18 to 34 Income Level: 18% over $100k/yr

So why is the above relevant?

Given that the majority of commercial real estate clients tend to be Male, between 45 and 60 with mid to high level six figure salaries we can see that it wouldn't be worth our time to advertise our Industrial or Office availabilities on a site that has a primary demographic of females between the ages of 12 and 17 such as is found at Bebo.com

Overall, LinkedIn seems to be the best site for professionals to connect with other professions, followed closely by Facebook, which also boasts 9 times the number of visitors and users when compared to LinkedIn. The only other site from this list I would consider, from a strictly commercial real estate point of view, would be Ning, as this social networking site operates completely different than the others. Instead of signing up and being part of a wide variety of users the site instead allows each user to create or subscribe to user driven social clubs. Essentially a Ning user can create their own "social networking group", such as a social club focusing on Las Vegas Real Estate.

While other social media services like Twitter can compliment all of these sites it may also be worthwhile to look at up and coming networks. Recently I became aware of a new social networking site geared specifically for real estate professionals. The site, RealCorner.com is still relatively new and unfortunately I could not find much third party information for them short of Alexa.com which of my last checking had a lot of holes to fill with their information still.

In any case the site is still worth watching and based on its description and meta tags is usually not blocked by most companies firewalls or web filters, much like LinkedIn, where as most of the popular sites listed above are blocked from within the work place.

Michael G. Hurston http://www.michaelghurston.com

Michael Hurston

Why Bother With Social Networking Sites Like LinkedIn?

Q: I think I understand the value of networking as well as the next businessman, but for the life of me, I don't really see what sites like LinkedIn, Ryze and Ecademy can do for me. What's the point of these sites other than just as some sort of digital popularity contest?

A: My good friend and colleague Liz Ryan, head of the women's power networking group WorldWIT, Women in Technology, has a great answer to this sort of question, an answer that I'm quoting here with permission:

I ask people to join LinkedIn, and often they say "I don't want the spam." So I say "You won't get any spam." And they say "But I'm not job-hunting." And I say "You don't have to be job-hunting." Then we go back and forth for awhile. It's a bit of a challenge to get my own friends to see the forest for the trees, sometimes. When Monster.com was new, the big idea was to post jobs online. As an HR person, I can tell you, Monster is a pretty awful place to post jobs. You get KILLED with unwanted resumes from job seekers all over the world. I truly believe that Monster.com is the reason that HR people no longer respond to online job seekers - and sometimes offline job seekers - with any kind of response.

Anyway, over time HR people and recruiters figured out that the real value to Monster is the ability to search the candidate database (for a fee). Maybe some of the same thing is happening with LinkedIn. What seems like the obvious benefit to membership may not be the key feature for a lot of users. See what you think about this LinkedIn primer that I share with my friends. If I'm doing something I shouldn't be doing on LinkedIn, I'd love to know that too!

1) Your profile itself is a great value to joining LinkedIn. I get great, useful contacts from my profile appearing on LI, and of course it's free.

2) Even if you're not job-hunting or doing business developing or searching for contacts yourself, it's a great thing to be able to be a conduit for your friends. They really appreciate that service that you can provide for them. Just the reconnect- with-an-old colleague bit is a godsend: where else can you do that online?

3) LinkedIn is the google for individuals who aren't high on Google rankings. That means anyone who's in a corporation but not senior enough to appear on the About Us/Management Bios page (although of course, those execs are often on LinkedIn too); anyone who is a partner in a consulting firm but perhaps not often in the news or otherwise mentioned online; and zillions of other people whom you'd have trouble finding if it weren't for LinkedIn.

4) Let's say you have a business meeting with the VP of Marketing at a major corporation next week. If it weren't for his profile on LinkedIn (say, if you were having this meeting three years ago), how would you learn where he went to school, where he worked before his current job, and other details about him? With the help of his LinkedIn profile, you're a zillion times better prepared for the meeting.

5) Now let's say that VP of Marketing is behind the curve and doesn't have a LinkedIn profile. No big; you find another connection of yours who works at the VP's current company, and ping her for some background. See? LinkedIn to the rescue again.

6) Want to know who's working in a particular industry space in a given city? LinkedIn search. Intelligence gathering, even if you never contact any of the people you find.

My point is that there's lots more to LinkedIn than just reaching out to people for job leads and for business development leads - not that either of those are bad things. And I agree with other posters that you have to use the tool, rather than just join up and sit there like a lump. But I'd love to hear stories of some more creative uses for LinkedIn, from other users...

Thanks for sharing your compelling story with everyone, Liz. When I think about your point with Monster.com causing recruiters to never list jobs online anymore, I not only know that it's true from personal experience, but also find it to be an interesting example of the law of unintended consequences, in the same way that a site like LinkedIn helps with market research or background checks.

At the end of the day, in business you're ultimately constrained only by the skills you can bring to the table and the network of friends and acquaintances you can call on for help, advice and assistance. And if you don't help them when you can, of course, it doesn't take long to be ostracized from a group, however informal or far-flung. But if you are part of a circle of professionals, you will always grow your career faster, smarter, and more profitably.

Dave Taylor is an internationally recognized expert on business and technical topics and is the author of 18 different books and thousands of magazine articles. His Q&A Web site is http://www.askdavetaylor.com/

Dave Taylor

Why Executive Job Seekers Need To Join The Social Networking Craze

It seems everyone is talking about social networking. Articles abound on how to use LinkedIn, Twitter, and Facebook for your job search.

Is this just a phase, or is social networking here to stay? Can executives actually find these tools useful or are they just for the new college grads?

Here are some compelling reasons for executives to incorporate these tools into their job searches:

The number of job postings has declined. According to Scripps News, "Despite the boom in traffic, many recruitment sites are taking a financial hit. Many charge employers to post openings, a far less frequent activity in these days of hiring freezes and layoffs.

Indeed.com, a major job board, found that there were 119,171 postings for the accounting industry in January, down 53 percent from a year earlier. Postings in technology were down 43 percent to 395,629. The sectors that held up the best were health care, which was down 8 percent to 581,625 postings, and education, in which postings fell 9 percent to 62,933." ("Traffic on Job Websites Jumps," Scripps News, March 13, 2009)

The amount of traffic to job boards has jumped. "With the unemployment rate rising to 8.1 percent nationwide, career sites are booming in popularity as users desperately look for work. Traffic to job search sites, for instance, grew 51 percent in January from the same month a year earlier, according to comScore Media Metrix." ("Traffic on Job Websites Jumps," Scripps News, March 13, 2009)

A large number of recruiters maintain a presence on social networking sites like LinkedIn. "LinkedIn has recently been adding a million new members every two weeks, and officials say more than 829,000 HR professionals and 521,000 corporate recruiters now use the network." ("LinkedIn Beefing Up Recruiting Tools," Workforce Management, January 9, 2009) With hundreds of thousands of recruiters on LinkedIn alone, executive candidates cannot afford not to use this tool to connect to people who are seeking to fill positions.

Increasingly recruiters are searching online for candidates instead of simply advertising jobs on job boards. According to MSNBC, "These days, small and midsize companies aren't even posting jobs, instead going to sites like LinkedIn in search of their ideal candidate.

("Using LinkedIn to Maximize Your Job Search," MSNBC.com, March 12, 2009)

And an organization called Organic explains it this way on Advertising Age: "Why are we weaning ourselves from traditional job boards? Simple: We get results from social-networking tools -- with no expense. Every day we discover new and innovative ways to use social media for our recruiting efforts. While Twitter and other social-media sites may seem like the flavor of the month, the real proof is in the numbers. In terms of return on investment, there is no investment besides time. From a branding perspective, it's always a win. Retweeting is easy and more far-reaching than a static posting a job on a traditional job board. With a solid social-networking strategy, most companies can reduce job-board spending quickly, while pinpointing discipline- or industry-specific candidates. ("Why Tweeting Has Become Organic's Main Job-Posting Strategy," Advertising Age, March 31, 2009)

Executive recruiters regularly search the Internet for additional information on executive candidates. "In a(n) . . . ExecuNet survey about reputation management and Internet presence, 86 percent of executive recruiters say they routinely scour online sources for information that goes beyond a candidate's rÃ©sumÃ©. Nearly 7-in-10 search firm consultants say that executive job candidates' prospects improve when positive information is found online." (2008 Executive Job Market Intelligence Report from ExecuNet)

Networking is a lifelong career strategy. The New York Times calls social networking your career safety net (The Social Network as a Career Safety Net, The New York Times, August 13, 2008). The Financial Post states it this way: "Maintain your presence online. Some people believe Facebook is destroying America. But if you lose your job, you'll probably lose e-mail addresses for all of your colleagues, and you'll need some way to stay in touch. As Kay Luo, a spokeswoman for LinkedIn advises, "Build your network before you need it." ("How to find a job online," Financial Post, March 20, 2009)

Cheryl Palmer, M.Ed. is a certified career coach and a professional resume writer. She has been a guest on a radio show entitled "How to Find a Job Fast" hosted by Chris Russell where she discussed tips for finding employment more quickly in this economic downturn. In addition, she was a guest on the radio show "Balance and Wisdom" where she discussed networking for your career with hosts Barbara Phillips and Joanie Winberg.

In an article on HotJobs' website entitled "The Art of Being Assertive," Cheryl was quoted as a subject matter expert on how assertiveness can help a person advance in his or her career. She was also quoted in an article on CNN: "What Says to an Employer, 'Hire Me!'"

Cheryl also has a background in training and curriculum design on career development topics. She does workshops on career choice and various aspects of the job search process such as resume writing, interviewing skills, and networking.

Cheryl Palmer

Why Telling People What You Do Too Soon Can Sabotage Your Networking

There are four words that when strung together are very dangerous - I already knew that. Most of us know when we're in a class or workshop it's best not to be wearing our expert hat, but did you know it applies to talking about what you do?

When you're out introducing yourself, remember that everyone you meet will be wearing their "expert hat" - their pre-conceived notion - about what your job title means. If you tell someone you are a financial planner for example, most people think they know what that is, decide from past experience whether it applies to something they care about, and walk away from you if it's not.

If, however you say something like, "I help baby boomer women achieve financial independence" (or something like that), your listeners "expert hat" will come right off because they won't understand exactly what that is.

Case in point. One of my students is a "holistic healer". She was at a networking event and someone asked her "what do you do?" Fresh out of the workshop she really wasn't sure what I taught her would actually work so she said, "I am a holistic healer". The person who she was talking to said, "Oh my gosh. My mother went to a holistic healer and they said she was going to die within a year!"

OK - End of conversation.

Most of us know that's not the kind of thing a holistic healer typically does. Her listener had a misconception about the title because of a bad experience. She had her "expert hat" on about what that profession meant, and since she was a bit traumatized by the experience, a further conversation would be problematic.

This same thing will happen to you no matter what your profession is if you introduce yourself and state your profession in the first two or three sentences.

If I told you I was a writer (which I am, by the way) what would you think?

Maybe I write romance novels, maybe newspaper columns or magazine ads. I wouldn't get to the part about what I actually do (teach people how to write and deliver elevator speeches). You would have already decided that I do what your "expert hat" has told you about what a writer does. You would have stopped listening and being curious because you thought you knew. Have you ever experienced this?

This is normal. We all do it (even me) and doesn't make you - or anyone else for that matter - a bad person. People are busy and have short attention spans. When we're at an event it's easy to be distractable.

Remember, when you introduce yourself to tell how you help people, who you help and who you are looking for. You'll meet allot of great people and maybe even get an introduction to your dream client!

Want to use this article in your newsletter or on your website? You can! Just be sure to include the entire article and include this complete "blurb" with it:

Networking Expert, Karen Frank publishes Networking News, a semi-monthly newsletter devoted to helping you avoid marketing disasters and networking faux pas. Get the home study course "The Seven Deadly Sins of Networking and How to Avoid them" Free when you sign up for Networking News at http://www.7deadlysinsofnetworking.com

Karen L Frank

You Have 0 Friends - The Lament of a Social Networking Outcast

You have 0 friends. That was the message I saw every morning for the two weeks I tried to set up a page on a social network. That's not good for a person with doubtful self-confidence. I removed myself without ever having had a single friend, or even figuring out how to get one.

Five years ago, I began writing mysteries. I didn't know then that the need to write would consume me, but what bliss to find myself overwhelmed by a new passion in my mid 50s--a time that can mark endings rather than beginnings if you allow it. After a few years of non-stop writing, I wanted to publish and found it more difficult than I'd thought. I had less time than a twenty-year old and with my years of training as a graphic artist, I decided to self-publish, an action also likely to make one a social outcast. Many in publishing do not think self-published authors really exist, or rather that they should exist. I won't go into what I think that's all about, but for me, the bottom line is that I want to write, I want to share what I've written, and I have begun to see that there are folks who want to read it. That works for me.

One thing became clear when I began self-publishing--the need to learn marketing. At this point in the evolution of the internet, that means social networking. I tried. I really did. I joined countless sites where I could expose my work and myself. I tubed, booked, spaced, and roomed. I blogged and responded to blogs. I read all the instructions the spaces offered to get the most exposure and every bit of advice I could ingest from the internet. When I quit the last one, I shook my head at the message. After all my efforts, I had four friends. I did better in the real world.

Here's my biggest problem with social networking. How can one do it well and still have a life, find time to do anything else, and maintain some semblance of sanity. I may be missing something very simple, but I can't make it work. The more hours I put in, the more frustrated I became and the less 'real' work I accomplished. I decided to return to my focus to writing, offer an occasional piece on EzineArticles, and spend some time with non-virtual types. It is much easier on my weary soul. Being a social outcast isn't that bad, some of my best friends don't have cell phones.

Born and raised in Chicago, Jean Sheldon now makes her home in Eugene, Oregon. She has published the first three books in her Chicago Police Detective Kerry Grant series, 'Identity Murder', 'Should Old Acquaintance be Dead', and 'A Chilling Goodbye'. She recently released 'The Woman in the Wing', an historical mystery about WWII women pilots and riveters.

Website: http://www.jeansheldon.com

Jean Sheldon

Your Networking Posse

If you have trouble getting motivated to get out and network, maybe you should consider developing your own Networking Posse. In fact, it can be one the best ways to create synergy and momentum.

Figure out how many people you would like to buddy up with and set a goal to attend at least 1-3 events per week. Each person should come up with at least 4 different places to go networking in the month. Create a central place to all meet up and then go together.

If you already have a sphere of influence that share a similar target audience as you do, why not join forces and network as a group?

You can all partner up after the event and each person share their contacts they made. For example, let's say you have four people in your Networking Posse and you all attend an event and each meet 10 people. If you all shared those contacts with each other, you would have 40 people that you, as a group, reached.

Although it would make sense to combine your contacts to leverage your time and multiple your efforts, I would not assume that these additional people want you to contact them. Instead, reference the other people in your posse that suggested that you follow up with them. Maybe tell them that you were referred by your posse and take it from there.

If you are all with the same company, you'll infiltrate the group and make a HUGE impact. Everyone at the meeting will take notice. I used to refer to this maneuver as sending in the S.W.A.T. team, S uccessful W omen A ttending T ogether!

The benefits of developing your networking posse are to have fun while you're marketing your business and producing incredible results.

Darlene Willman, aka The Sassy Networker, is a keynote speaker , author and coach, specializing in small business networking and referrals. She provides resources, connections and support to entrepreneurs, small business owners and other professionals that have a strong desire to promote their companies through relationship marketing. She will show you how to build an incredible network of people who refer business to each other plus so much more. You can start receiving her eZine, The Networking Focus (a $67 value) by visiting http://www.SassyNetworker.com

Contact our office today at (636) 387-3000 to book Darlene Willman as your next keynote speaker.

Darlene Willman

INDEX*

C

O

P

Lightning Source UK Ltd.
Milton Keynes UK
01 March 2011

168478UK00001B/74/P

9 781742 441603